Anonymous

The Southern Methodist Hymn and Tune Book

A collection of the best and most popular hymns and tunes, for public and family

worship

Anonymous

The Southern Methodist Hymn and Tune Book
A collection of the best and most popular hymns and tunes, for public and family worship

ISBN/EAN: 9783337290337

Printed in Europe, USA, Canada, Australia, Japan

Cover: Foto ©Thomas Meinert / pixelio.de

More available books at **www.hansebooks.com**

THE

'SOUTHERN METHODIST

HYMN AND TUNE BOOK.

A COLLECTION

OF

THE BEST AND MOST POPULAR

HYMNS AND TUNES,

FOR

Public and Family Worship.

———o०঎०o———

MACON AND ATLANTA, GA.:
J. W. BURKE & CO.
1875.

PREFACE.

THIS "Hymn and Tune Book" is published to meet the demand for a low-priced book containing Hymns and Tunes adapted to congregational singing in Methodist Churches. The Hymns are those which are most commonly used in Public and Social worship.

The Tunes are those familiar and favorite airs which general use for many years has endorsed.

The book is offered to Methodist congregations with the fervent prayer that it may become the means of reviving the old love of sacred song, and of restoring "the former times" of spirited and spiritual congregational singing.

☞ The black type used in numbering of Hymns shows corresponding hymn in the Hymn-Book.

iii

INDEX OF METRES.

ORDER OF ARRANGEMENT AND INDEX OF TUNES.

1 *

INDEX OF HYMNS.

SOUTHERN METHODIST
HYMN AND TUNE BOOK.

CAMBRIDGE. C. M. RANDALL.

1 (1)   C. M.   C. WESLEY.
The Trinity.

A THOUSAND oracles Divine
Their common beams unite,
That sinners may with angels join
To worship God aright:

2 To praise a Trinity adored
By all the hosts above;
And one thrice holy God and Lord
Through endless ages love.

3 Triumphant host! they never cease
To laud and magnify
The Triune God of holiness,
Whose glory fills the sky:

4 Whose glory to this earth extends,
When God himself imparts,
And the whole Trinity descends
Into our faithful hearts.

5 By faith the upper choir we meet,
And challenge them to sing
Jehovah on his shining seat,
Our Maker and our King.

2 (14)   C. M.   C. WESLEY.
Divine Excellence.

HAIL, Father, Son, and Holy Ghost
One God in persons three:
Of thee we make our joyful boast,
Our songs we make of thee!

2 Thou neither canst be felt nor seen,
Thou art a spirit pure:
Thou from eternity hast been,
And always shalt endure.

3 Present alike in every place,
Thy Godhead we adore:
Beyond the bounds of time and space
Thou dwell'st for evermore.

4 In wisdom infinite thou art,
Thine eye doth all things see;
And every thought of every heart
Is fully known to thee.

5 Whate'er thou wilt, in earth below
Thou dost, in heaven above;
But chiefly we rejoice to know
Th' almighty God of love.

9

KENTUCKY. S. M.

3 (7)   S. M.   C. WESLEY.

The Trinity.

FATHER, in whom we live,
In whom we are and move,
The glory, power, and praise receive,
Of thy creating love.

2 Let all the angel throng
Give thanks to God on high,
While earth repeats the joyful song,
And echoes through the sky.

3 Incarnate Deity,
Let all the ransomed race
Render, in thanks, their lives to thee,
For thy redeeming grace:

4 The grace to sinners showed,
Ye heavenly choirs proclaim,
And cry, "Salvation to our God,
Salvation to the Lamb!"

5 Spirit of holiness,
Let all thy saints adore
Thy sacred energy, and bless
Thy heart-renewing power.

4 (95)   S. M.   C. WESLEY.

"Unto us a child is born."

FATHER, our hearts we lift
Up to thy gracious throne,
And thank thee for the precious gift
Of thine incarnate Son!

2 The gift unspeakable
We thankfully receive,
And to the world thy goodness tell,
And to thy glory live.

3 Jesus, the holy child,
Doth, by his birth, declare
That God and man are reconciled,
And one in him we are.

4 A peace on earth he brings,
Which never more shall end;
The Lord of hosts, the King of kings,
Declares himself our friend.

5 His kingdom from above
He doth to us impart,
And pure benevolence and love
O'erflow the faithful heart.

ROCKINGHAM. L. M.

5 **(15)**   L. M.   J. WESLEY.

The Glory of God.

O GOD, thou bottomless abyss!
  Thee to perfection who can know?
O height immense! What words suffice
  Thy countless attributes to show?

2 Unfathomable depths thou art!
  O plunge me in thy mercy's sea!
Void of true wisdom is my heart:
  With love embrace and cover me!

3 While thee, all infinite, I set,
  By faith, before my ravished eye,
My weakness bends beneath the weight:
  O'erpowered, I sink, I faint, I die.

4 Eternity thy fountain was,
  Which, like thee, no beginning knew:
Thou wast ere time began his race,
  Ere glowed with stars th'ethereal blue.

5 Greatness unspeakable is thine,
  Greatness, whose undiminished ray,
When short-lived worlds are lost, shall
    shine
  When earth and heaven are fled away.

6 **(21)**   L. M.   WATTS.

Divine Majesty.

ETERNAL Power, whose high abode
  Becomes the grandeur of a God:
Infinite lengths, beyond the bounds
Where stars revolve their little rounds.

2 Thee while the first archangel sings,
He hides his face beneath his wings,
And ranks of shining thrones around
Fall worshipping, and spread the ground.

3 Lord, what shall earth and ashes do?
We would adore our Maker too!
From sin and dust to thee we cry,
The Great, the Holy, and the High!

4 Earth from afar hath heard thy fame,
  And worms have learned to lisp thy
    name;
But O! the glories of thy mind
Leave all our soaring thoughts behind!

5 God is in heaven, and men below:
Be short our tunes; our words be few!
A solemn rev'rence checks our songs,
And praise sits silent on our tongues.

HEBRON. L. M.

Slow and soft.

7 (6) L. M. WATTS.
The Trinity.

BLEST be the Father, and his love,
　To whose celestial source we owe
Rivers of endless joy above,
　And rills of comfort here below.

2 Glory to Thee, great Son of God!
　From whose dear wounded body rolls
A precious stream of vital blood,
　Pardon and life for dying souls.

3 We give thee, sacred Spirit, praise,
　Who, in our hearts of sin and woe,
Mak'st living springs of grace arise,
　And into boundless glory flow.

4 Thus God the Father, God the Son,
　And God the Spirit, we adore:
That sea of life and love unknown,
　Without a bottom or a shore.

8 (18) L. M. J. WESLEY.
Providence.

PARENT of good! thy bounteous
　　hand
Incessant benefits distils:
　And all in air, or sea, or land,
　With plenteous food and gladness fills.

2 All things in thee live, move, and are,
　Thy power infused doth all sustain:
E'en those thy daily favors share
　Who, thankless, spurn thy easy reign.

3 Thy sun thou bidd'st his genial ray
　Alike on all impartial pour:
On all who hate or bless thy sway,
　Thou bidd'st descend the fruitful
　　shower.

4 Yet while, at length, who scorned thy
　　might
　Shall feel thee a consuming fire,
How sweet the joys, the crown how
　　bright,
　Of those who to thy love aspire!

9 (39) L. M.
The God of all Grace.

ETERNAL depth of love divine,
　In Jesus, God with us, displayed,
How bright thy beaming glories shine!
　How wide thy healing streams are
　　spread!

2 With whom dost thou delight to dwell?
　Sinners, a vile and thankless race;
O God! what tongue aright can tell
　How vast thy love, how great thy grace?

3 The dictates of thy sovereign will
　With joy our grateful hearts receive;
All thy delight in us fulfil;
　Lo! all we are to thee we give.

4 To thy sure love, thy tender care,
　Our flesh, soul, spirit, we resign;
O fix thy sacred presence there,
　And seal th' abode for ever thine.

BOYLSTON. S. M.

10 (28)   S. M.   Montgomery.

" Fearful in praises."

STAND up, and bless the Lord,
    Ye people of his choice:
Stand up, and bless the Lord your
    God,
  With heart, and soul, and voice.

2 Though high above all praise,
    Above all blessing high,
Who would not fear his holy name,
  And laud, and magnify?

3 O for the living flame
    From his own altar brought,
To touch our lips -- our minds inspire,
  And wing to heaven our thought!

4 There, with benign regard,
    Our hymns he deigns to hear:
Though unrevealed to mortal sense,
  The spirit feels him near.

5 God is our strength and song,
    And his salvation ours:
Then be his love in Christ proclaimed
  With all our ransomed powers.
  2

11 (20)   S. M.   C. Wesley.

Glory of God.

O ALL-CREATING God,
    At whose supreme decree
Our body rose, a breathing clod,
  Our souls sprang forth from thee:

2 For this thou hast designed,
    And formed us man for this:
To know and love thyself, and find
  In thee our endless bliss.

12 (61)   S. M.   Watts.

Psalm ciii. 8-12.

MY soul, repeat his praise,
    Whose mercies are so great;
Whose anger is so slow to rise,
  So ready to abate.

2 God will not always chide;
    And when his strokes are felt,
His strokes are fewer than our crimes,
  And lighter than our guilt.

3 High as the heavens are raised
    Above the ground we tread,
So far the riches of his grace
  Our highest thoughts exceed.

4 His power subdues our sins;
    And his forgiving love,
Far as the east is from the west,
  Doth all our guilt remove.

OLD HUNDRED. L. M.

13 (45)   L. M.   C. Wesley.

Opening Worship.

O THOU, whom all thy saints adore,
  We now with all thy saints agree,
And bow our inmost souls before
  Thy glorious, awful majesty.

2 The King of nations we proclaim:
  Who would not our great Sovereign
    fear?
We long t' experience all thy name,
  And now we come to meet thee here.

3 We come, great God, to seek thy face,
  And for thy loving-kindness wait:
And O, how dreadful is this place!
  'T is God's own house, 't is heaven's
    gate!

4 Tremble our hearts to find thee nigh,
  To thee our trembling hearts aspire;
And lo! we see descend from high
  The pillar and the flame of fire.

5 Still let it on th' assembly stay,
  And all the house with glory fill,
To Canaan's bounds point out the way,
  And lead us to thy holy hill.

14 (59)   L. M.   Watts.

Psalm c.

BEFORE Jehovah's awful throne,
  Ye nations bow with sacred joy:
Know that the Lord is God alone,
  He can create, and he destroy.

2 His sovereign power, without our aid,
  Made us of clay, and formed us
    men;
And when, like wandering sheep, we
    strayed,
  He brought us to his fold again.

3 We'll crowd thy gates with thankful
    songs,
High as the heavens our voices raise;
  And earth, with her ten thousand
    tongues,
Shall fill thy courts with sounding
    praise.

4 Wide as the world is thy command:
  Vast as eternity thy love:
Firm as a rock thy truth must stand,
  When rolling years shall cease to
    move.

15 (26)　S. M.

All-sufficiency.

MY God, my life, my love,
　To thee, to thee I call:
I cannot live if thou remove,
For thou art all in all.

2 Thy shining grace can cheer
　This dungeon where I dwell:
'T is paradise when thou art here,
　If thou depart, 't is hell.

3 The smilings of thy face,
　How amiable they are!
'T is heaven to rest in thine embrace,
　And nowhere else but there.

4 To thee, and thee alone,
　The angels owe their bliss;
They sit around thy gracious throne,
　And dwell where Jesus is.

5 Not all the harps above
　Can make a heavenly place,
If God his residence remove,
　Or' but conceal his face.

16 (924)　C. M.　　C. WESLEY.

For the Divine fulness.

BEING of beings, God of love,
　To thee our hearts we raise;
Thy all-sustaining power we prove,
And gladly sing thy praise.

2 Thine, wholly thine, we pant to be,
　Our sacrifice receive;
Made, and preserved, and saved by thee,
　To thee ourselves we give.

3 Heavenward our every wish aspires,
　For all thy mercy's store;
The sole return thy love requires
　Is, that we ask for more.

4 For more we ask; we open then
　Our hearts t' embrace thy will;
Turn, and beget us, Lord, again;
　With all thy fulness fill.

5 Come, Holy Ghost, the Saviour's love
　Shed in our hearts abroad;
So shall we ever live and move
　And be with Christ in God.

17 (37)　C. M.　　HERVEY.

Too wise to err — too good to be unkind.

SINCE all the varying scenes of time
　God's watchful eye surveys,
O, who so wise to choose our lot,
　Or to appoint our ways!

2 Good when he gives—supremely good—
　Nor less when he denies:
E'en crosses, from his sovereign hand,
　Are blessings in disguise.

3 Why should we doubt a Father's love,
　So constant and so kind?
To his unerring, gracious will,
　Be every wish resigned.

18 (41)　C. M.　　C. WESLEY.

Exodus xxxiv. 6, 7.

THY ceaseless, unexhausted love,
　Unmerited and free,
Delights our evil to remove,
　And help our misery.

2 Thou waitest to be gracious still,
　Thou dost with sinners bear,
That, saved, we may thy goodness feel,
　And all thy grace declare.

3 Thy goodness and thy truth to me,
　To every soul, abound:
A vast unfathomable sea,
　Where all our thoughts are drowned.

4 Its streams the whole creation reach,
　So plenteous is the store:
Enough for all, enough for each,
　Enough for evermore.

19 (34)　C. M.　　C. WESLEY.

1 Chron. xxix. 10–13.

BLEST be our everlasting Lord,
　Our Father, God, and King!
Thy sovereign goodness we record,
　Thy glorious power we sing.

2 By thee the victory is given:
　The majesty Divine,
And strength, and might, and earth, and
　heaven,
And all therein, are thine.

3 The kingdom, Lord, is thine alone,
　Who dost thy right maintain;
And, high on thy eternal throne,
　O'er men and angels reign.

STONEFIELD. L. M.   STANLEY.

20 (55) L. M.   WATTS.

Psalm xxxvi. 5–9.

HIGH in the heavens, eternal God,
  Thy goodness in full glory shines:
Thy truth shall break through every
    cloud
  That veils and darkens thy designs.

2 For ever firm thy justice stands,
    As mountains their foundations keep:
  Wise are the wonders of thy hands:
    Thy judgments are a mighty deep.

3 Thy providence is kind and large,
    Both man and beast thy bounty share:
  The whole creation is thy charge,
    But saints are thy peculiar care.

4 My God! how excellent thy grace!
    Whence all our hope and comfort
        springs:
  The sons of Adam in distress
    Fly to the shadow of thy wings.

5 Life, like a fountain, rich and free,
    Springs from the presence of the Lord;
  And in thy light our souls shall see
    The glories promised in thy word.

21 (227) L. M.   WATTS.

Psalm xlvi. 1–5.

GOD is the refuge of his saints,
  When storms of sharp distress in-
    vade;
Ere we can offer our complaints,
  Behold him present with his aid.

2 Let mountains from their seats be hurled
    Down to the deep, and buried there—
  Convulsions shake the solid world—
    Our faith shall never yield to fear.

3 Loud may the troubled ocean roar—
    In sacred peace our souls abide;
  While every nation, every shore,
    Trembles, and dreads the swelling tide.

4 There is a stream, whose gentle flow
    Supplies the city of our God;
  Life, love, and joy, still gliding through,
    And wat'ring our divine abode.

5 That sacred stream, thy holy word,
    Our grief allays, our fear controls:
  Sweet peace thy promises afford,
    And give new strength to fainting
        souls.

22 (56)   C. M.   WATTS.
Psalm lxiii.   Opening Morning Service.

EARLY, my God, without delay,
   I haste to seek thy face:
My thirsty spirit faints away,
   Without thy cheering grace.

2 So pilgrims, on the scorching sand,
   Beneath a burning sky,
Long for a cooling stream at hand;
   And they must drink or die.

3 I 've seen thy glory and thy power
   Through all thy temple shine:
My God, repeat that heavenly hour,
   That vision so divine.

4 Not all the blessings of a feast
   Can please my soul so well,
As when thy richer grace I taste,
   And in thy presence dwell.

23 (57)   S. M.
Psalm xcv.   Opening Worship.

COME, sound his praise abroad,
   And hymns of glory sing;
Jehovah is the sovereign God,
   The universal King.

2 He formed the deep unknown;
   He gave the seas their bound;
The watery worlds are all his own,
   And all the solid ground.

3 Come, worship at his throne;
   Come, bow before the Lord;
We are his work, and not our own,
   He formed us by his word.

4 To-day attend his voice,
   Nor dare provoke his rod;
Come, like the people of his choice,
   And own your gracious God.

24 (71)   C. M.   WATTS.
Psalm cxlv.

LET every tongue thy goodness speak,
   Thou sovereign Lord of all :
Thy strengthening hands uphold the
     weak,
   And raise the poor that fall.

2 When sorrows bow the spirit down,
   When virtue lies distressed,
   2 *

Beneath the proud oppressor's frown,
   Thou giv'st the mourner rest.

3 Thou know'st the pains thy servants feel,
   Thou hear'st thy children's cry;
And their best wishes to fulfil,
   Thy grace is ever nigh.

4 Thy mercy never shall remove
   From men of heart sincere:
Thou sav'st the souls whose humble love
   Is joined with holy fear.

25 (62)   S. M.   WATTS.
Psalm ciii. 13–18.

THE pity of the Lord,
   To those that fear his name,
Is such as tender parents feel :
   He knows our feeble frame.

2 He knows we are but dust,
   Scattered with every breath :
His anger, like a rising wind,
   Can send us swift to death.

3 Our days are as the grass,
   Or like the morning flower:
If one sharp blast sweep o'er the field,
   It withers in an hour.

4 But thy compassions, Lord,
   To endless years endure;
And children's children ever find
   Thy words of promise sure.

26 (53)   S. M.   WATTS.
Psalm xxiii.

THE Lord my Shepherd is,
   I shall be well supplied :
Since he is mine, and I am his,
   What can I want beside ?

2 He leads me to the place
   Where heavenly pasture grows,
Where living waters gently pass,
   And full salvation flows.

3 If e'er I go astray,
   He doth my soul reclaim,
And guides me in his own right way,
   For his most holy name.

4 While he affords his aid,
   I cannot yield to fear :
Though I should walk through death's
     dark shade,
   My Shepherd 's with me there.

SUDBURY. 7s.

T. CLARK.

---

27 (68). 7s.

Psalm cxxxvi.

LET us, with a gladsome mind,
  Praise the Lord, for he is kind:
For his mercies aye endure,
Ever faithful, ever sure.

2 Let us blaze his name abroad,
For of gods he is the God;
For his mercies aye endure,
Ever faithful, ever sure.

3 All things living he doth feed;
His full hand supplies their need:
For his mercies aye endure,
Ever faithful, ever sure.

4 Let us therefore warble forth
His high majesty and worth:
For his mercies aye endure,
Ever faithful, ever sure.

Doxology.

Sing we to our God above,
Praise eternal as his love;
Praise him, all ye heavenly host—
Father, Son, and Holy Ghost.

---

28 (312) 7s.   C. WESLEY.

Gloria in Excelsis.

GLORY be to God on high,
  God whose glory fills the sky;
Peace on earth to man forgiven,
Man, the well-beloved of Heaven.

2 Sovereign Father, heavenly King,
Thee we now presume to sing;
Glad thine attributes confess,
Glorious all, and numberless.

3 Hail, by all thy works adored!
Hail, the everlasting Lord!
Thee with thankful hearts we prove,
Lord of power, and God of love.

4 Christ our Lord and God we own,
Christ the Father's only Son;
Lamb of God for sinners slain,
Saviour of offending man.

5 Bow thine ear, in mercy bow,
Hear, the world's atonement, thou!
Jesus, in thy name we pray,
Take, O take our sins away!

GENEVA. C. M.

J. COLE.

29 **(69)** C. M. WATTS.

Psalm cxxxix. 1-6.

LORD, all I am is known to thee:
　In vain my soul would try
To shun thy presence, or to flee
　The notice of thine eye.

2 Thy all-surrounding sight surveys
　My rising and my rest,
My public walks, my private ways,
　The secrets of my breast.

3 My thoughts lie open to thee, Lord,
　Before they 're formed within,
And ere my lips pronounce the word,
　Thou know'st the sense I mean.

4 O wondrous knowledge! deep and high:
　Where can a creature hide?
Within thy circling arms I lie,
　Beset on every side.

5 So let thy grace surround me still,
　And like a bulwark prove,
To guard my soul from every ill,
　Secured by sovereign love.

Doxology.

Now let the Father, and the Son,
　And Spirit be adored,　　[known,
Where there are works to make him
　Or saints to love the Lord.

30 **(35)** C. M. COWPER.

" Wonderful in counsel."

GOD moves in a mysterious way
　His wonders to perform:
He plants his footsteps in the sea,
　And rides upon the storm.

2 Deep in unfathomable mines
　Of never-failing skill,
He treasures up his bright designs,
　And works his sovereign will.

3 Ye fearful saints, fresh courage take:
　The clouds ye so much dread
Are big with mercy, and shall break
　In blessings on your head.

4 Judge not the Lord by feeble sense,
　But trust him for his grace:
Behind a frowning providence
　He hides a smiling face.

5 His purposes will ripen fast,
　Unfolding every hour:
The bud may have a bitter taste,
　But sweet will be the flower.

6 Blind unbelief is sure to err,
　And scan his work in vain:
God is his own interpreter,
　And he will make it plain.

31 (99) C. M. WATTS.
Psalm xcviii.

JOY to the world — the Lord is come!
Let earth receive her King:
Let every heart prepare him room,
And heaven and nature sing.

2 Joy to the earth — the Saviour reigns!
Let men their songs employ;
While fields and floods, rocks, hills, and
plains,
Repeat the sounding joy.

3 No more let sins and sorrows grow,
Nor thorns infest the ground:
He comes to make his blessings flow,
Far as the curse is found.

4 He rules the world with truth and grace;
And makes the nations prove
The glories of his righteousness,
And wonders of his love.

32 (89) 7s. C. WESLEY.
The Incarnation.

HARK! the herald angels sing,
"Glory to the new-born King;
Peace on earth, and mercy mild;
God and sinners reconciled:"
Joyful all ye nations rise,
Join the triumphs of the skies;
With th' angelic hosts proclaim,
"Christ is born in Bethlehem."

2 Christ, by highest heaven adored,
Christ, the everlasting Lord:
Late in time behold him come,
Offspring of a virgin's womb,
Veiled in flesh the Godhead see,
Hail th' incarnate Deity!
Pleased as man with men t' appear,
Jesus our Immanuel here.

3 Hail, the heaven-born Prince of peace!
Hail, the Sun of righteousness!
Light and life to all he brings,
Risen with healing in his wings:
Mild he lays his glory by,
Born that man no more may die;
Born to raise the sons of earth;
Born to give them second birth.

4 Come, Desire of nations, come!
Fix in us thy humble home:
Rise, the woman's conqu'ring Seed,
Bruise in us the serpent's head:

Adam's likeness now efface,
Stamp thine image in its place:
Second Adam from above,
Reinstate us in thy love.

33 (114) S. M. C. WESLEY.
" My soul is exceeding sorrowful."

THE man of sorrow now
Thou dost indeed appear,—
Beneath my guilty burden bow,
And tremble with my fear.

2 Thy pain is my relief,
And doth my load remove;
For O, if all thy soul is grief,
Yet all thy heart is love!

34 (178) 8s, 7s. ROBINSON.
Praise to the Redeemer.

MIGHTY God, while angels bless thee,
May a mortal lisp thy name?
Lord of men, as well as angels,
Thou art every creature's theme.

2 Lord of every land and nation,
Ancient of eternal days!
Sounded through the wide creation
Be thy just and lawful praise.

3 For the grandeur of thy nature —
Grand beyond a seraph's thought —
For created works of power,
Works with skill and kindness
wrought:

4 For thy providence that governs
Through thine empire's wide domain:
Wings an angel — guides a sparrow —
Blessed be thy gentle reign.

5 But thy rich, thy free redemption,
Dark through brightness all along!
Thought is poor, and poor expression:
Who dare sing that awful song?

6 Brightness of the Father's glory,
Shall thy praise unuttered lie?
Fly, my tongue, such guilty silence!
Sing the Lord who came to die.

7 Did archangels sing thy coming?
Did the shepherds learn their lays?
Shame would cover me, ungrateful,
Should my tongue refuse to praise.

WEBB. 7s & 6s.

G. J. WEBB.

35 **(742)** 7s, 6s.

Psalm lxxii. 1–11.

HAIL to the Lord's Anointed,
Great David's greater Son!
Hail, in the time appointed,
His reign on earth begun!
He comes to break oppression,
To let the captive free,
To take away transgression,
And rule in equity.

2 He comes, with succor speedy,
To those who suffer wrong;
To help the poor and needy,
And bid the weak be strong;
To give them songs for sighing,
Their darkness turn to light,
Whose souls, condemned and dying,
Were precious in his sight.

3 He shall come down like showers,
Upon the fruitful earth,

And love, joy, hope, like flowers,
Spring in his path to birth:
Before him on the mountains,
Shall peace the herald go;
And righteousness in fountains
From hill to valley flow.

4 Arabia's desert-ranger
To him shall bow the knee;
The Ethiopian stranger
His glory come to see:
With off'rings of devotion,
Ships from the isles shall meet,
To pour the wealth of ocean,
In tribute, at his feet.

5 Kings shall fall down before him,
And gold and incense bring;
All nations shall adore him,
His praise all people sing:
For he shall have dominion
O'er river, sea, and shore,
Far as the eagle's pinion,
Or dove's light wing can soar.

GREENVILLE. 8s, 7s, & 4s.

36 (934) 8s, 7s.

" Come, Lord Jesus."

COME, thou long-expected Jesus,
  Born to set thy people free;
From our fears and sins release us,
  Let us find our rest in thee:

2 Israel's Strength and Consolation,
  Hope of all the earth thou art, —
Dear Desire of every nation,
  Joy of every longing heart.

3 Born thy people to deliver;
  Born a child, and yet a King;
Born to reign in us for ever,
  Now thy gracious kingdom bring:

4 By thine own Eternal Spirit,
  Rule in all our hearts alone;
By thine all-sufficient merit,
  Raise us to thy glorious throne.

Doxology.

Praise the Father, earth, and heaven,
  Praise the Son, the Spirit praise,
As it was, and is, be given,
  Glory through eternal days.

37 (941) 8s, 7s.   NEWTON.

" Lord, revive us."

SAVIOUR, visit thy plantation,
  Grant us, Lord, a gracious rain!
All will come to desolation,
  Unless thou return again.
Chorus. Lord, revive us; Lord, revive us;
  All our help must come from thee.

2 Keep no longer at a distance,
  Shine upon us from on high,
Lest, for want of thy assistance,
  Every plant should droop and die.
  Lord, revive us, etc.

3 Surely once thy garden flourished,
  Every plant looked gay and green;
Then thy word our spirits nourished —
  Happy seasons we have seen.
  Lord, revive us, etc.

4 But a drought has since succeeded,
  And a sad decline we see;
Lord, thy help is greatly needed,
  Help can only come from thee.
  Lord, revive us, etc.

38 (104) L. M. BOWRING.
The Great Teacher.

HOW sweetly flowed the gospel sound
From lips of gentleness and grace,
When list'ning thousands gathered
round,
And joy and gladness filled the place!

2 From heaven he came, of heaven he
spoke,
To heaven he led his foll'wers' way :
Dark clouds of gloomy night he broke,
Unveiling an immortal day.

3 "Come, wand'rers, to my Father's home;
Come, all ye weary ones, and rest:"
Yes, sacred Teacher, we will come,
Obey thee, love thee, and be blest.

39 (105) L. M. WATTS.
His Exemplary Life.

MY dear Redeemer, and my Lord,
I read my duty in thy word ;
But in thy life the law appears,
Drawn out in living characters.

2 Such was thy truth, and such thy zeal,
Such def'rence to thy Father's will,
Such love, and meekness so divine,
I would transcribe, and make them mine.

3 Cold mountains, and the midnight air,
Witnessed the fervor of thy prayer :
The desert thy temptations knew,
Thy conflict, and thy vict'ry too.

4 Be thou my pattern : make me bear
More of thy gracious image here ;
Then God, the Judge, shall own my
name,
Among the foll'wers of the Lamb.

40 (143) C. M.
He is risen.

YE humble souls, that seek the Lord,
Chase all your fears away ;
And bow with pleasure down to see
The place where Jesus lay.

2 Thus low the Lord of life was brought,
Such wonders love can do :
Thus cold in death that bosom lay,
Which throbbed and bled for you.

3 But raise your eyes, and tune your songs,
The Saviour lives again ;
Not all the bolts and bars of death
The Conqu'ror could detain.

4 High o'er th' angelic bands he rears
His once dishonored head ;
And through unnumbered years he
reigns,
Who dwelt among the dead.

5 With joy like his shall every saint
His empty tomb survey ;
Then rise with his ascending Lord,
Through all his shining way.

41 (152) C. M. DODDRIDGE.
Priesthood of Christ.

NOW let our cheerful eyes survey
Our great High-Priest above ;
And celebrate his constant care,
And sympathetic love.

2 Though raised to a superior throne,
Where angels bow around,
And high o'er all the shining train,
With matchless honors crowned, —

3 The names of all his saints he bears,
Deep graven on his heart ;
Nor shall the meanest Christian say
That he hath lost his part.

4 Those characters shall fair abide,
Our everlasting trust,
When gems and monuments and crowns
Are mouldered down to dust.

42 (181) L. M. WATTS.
Rev. i. 5, 6.

NOW to the Lord, who makes us know
The wonders of his dying love,
Be humble honors paid below,
And strains of nobler praise above.

2 'T was he who cleansed our foulest sins,
And washed us in his richest blood :
'T is he who makes us priests and kings,
And brings us rebels near to God.

3 To Jesus, our atoning Priest,
To Jesus, our superior King,
Be everlasting power confessed —
Let every tongue his glory sing.

ST. MARTINS. C. M.

TANSUR.

43 (106) C. M.   ENFIELD.

"I have given you an example."

BEHOLD where, in a mortal form,
    Appears each grace divine!
The virtues, all in Jesus met,
    With mildest radiance shine.

2 To spread the rays of heavenly light,
    To give the mourner joy,
To preach glad tidings to the poor,
    Was his divine employ.

3 Lowly in heart, to all his friends
    A friend and servant found:
He washed their feet, he wiped their
        tears,
    And healed each bleeding wound.

4 Midst keen reproach and cruel scorn,
    Patient and meek he stood:
His foes, ungrateful, sought his life:
    He labored for their good.

Doxology.

Now let the Father, and the Son,
    And Spirit be adored,   [known,
Where there are works to make him
    Or saints to love the Lord.

44 (197) C. M.   DODDRIDGE.

"He is precious."

JESUS, I love thy charming name,
    'T is music to my ear;
Fain would I sound it out so loud
    That earth and heaven should hear.

2 Yes, thou art precious to my soul,
    My transport and my trust;
Jewels, to thee, are gaudy toys,
    And gold is sordid dust.

3 All my capacious powers can wish,
    In thee doth richly meet;
Nor to mine eyes is light so dear,
    Nor friendships half so sweet.

4 Thy grace still dwells upon my heart,
    And sheds its fragrance there;
The noblest balm of all its wounds,
    The cordial of its care.

5 I'll speak the honors of thy name
    With my last, lab'ring breath!
Then speechless clasp thee in mine
        arms,
    The antidote of death.

TRURO. L. M.

BURNEY.

45 (117) L. M.   C. WESLEY.

Sufferings of Christ.

O THOU dear suff'ring Son of God,
  How doth thy heart to sinners move!
Help me to catch thy precious blood !
Help me to taste thy dying love !

2 The earth could to her centre quake,
  Convulsed while her Creator died :
O let my inmost nature shake,
  And die with Jesus crucified !

3 At thy last gasp the graves displayed
  Their horrors to the upper skies :
O that my soul might burst the shade,
  And, quickened by thy death, arise !

4 The rocks could feel thy powerful death,
  And tremble, and asunder part :
O rend with thine expiring breath
  The harder marble of my heart !

46 (121) L. M.   J. WESLEY.

[From the German of Dessler.]

The Crucifixion.

EXTENDED on a cursed tree,
  Besmeared with dust, and sweat,
    and blood,

3

See there, the King of glory see !
Sinks, and expires, the Son of God !

2 Who, who, my Saviour, this hath done ?
  Who could thy sacred body wound ?
No guilt thy spotless heart hath known,
  No guile hath in thy lips been found.

3 I, — I alone have done the deed !
  'Tis I thy sacred flesh have torn :
My sins have caused thee, Lord, to bleed,
  Pointed the nail, and fixed the thorn.

4 For me, the burden, to sustain
  Too great, on thee, my Lord, was laid :
To heal me, thou hast borne the pain ;
  To bless me, thou a curse wast made.

5 In the devouring lion's teeth,
  Torn, and forsook of all, I lay :
Thou sprang'st into the jaws of death,
  From death to save the helpless prey.

6 My Saviour, how shall I proclaim,
  How pay the mighty debt I owe ?
Let all I have and all I am,
  Ceaseless to all thy glory show.

7 Too much to thee I cannot give ;
  Too much I cannot do for thee :
Let all thy love, and all thy grief,
  Grav'n on my heart for ever be !

MOZART. L. M.   ARRANGED.

47 (119) L. M. J. CHANDLER.

The Cross.

WHILE, in the agonies of death,
The Saviour yields his latest breath,
We, too, will mount on Calv'ry's height,
And contemplate the wondrous sight!

2 O Lamb of God, by faith we see
How all our hopes are fixed on thee:
Thy cross we see ordained by Heaven,
For man to look, and be forgiven.

3 By this thy saints to glory come;
By this they brave the martyr's doom;
In this the surest proof we find
Of God's vast love to lost mankind.

4 On this, O Lord, enthroned on high,
With more than royal majesty,
Thou spreadest forth thine arms abroad,
And callest all mankind to God.

5 O grant us then to find a place
Around the footstool of thy grace;
And there in humble faith to stay,
Till all our sins are washed away!

6 O, banner of the cross, unfurled
To shine with glory through the world,
O may we ever cleave to thee,
And thou shalt our salvation be!

48 (126) L. M.   WATTS.

Gal. vi. 14.

WHEN I survey the wondrous cross
On which the Prince of glory died,
My richest gain I count but loss,
And pour contempt on all my pride.

2 Forbid it, Lord, that I should boast,
Save in the death of Christ, my God;
All the vain things that charm me most,
I sacrifice them to his blood.

3 See, from his head, his hands, his feet,
Sorrow and love flow mingled down!
Did e'er such love and sorrow meet?
Or thorns compose so rich a crown?

4 Were the whole realm of nature mine,
That were a present far too small;
Love so amazing, so divine,
Demands my soul, my life, my all.

BELIEF. C. M.

49 (123) C. M.

The Crucifixion.

BEHOLD the Saviour of mankind
  Nailed to the shameful tree!
How vast the love that him inclined
  To bleed and die for thee!

2 Hark, how he groans! while nature
     shakes,
  And earth's strong pillars bend!
The temple's veil in sunder breaks,
  The solid marbles rend.

3 'T is done! the precious ransom's paid!
  " Receive my soul!" he cries:
See where he bows his sacred head!
  He bows his head, and dies!

4 But soon he'll break death's envious
     chain,
  And in full glory shine:
O Lamb of God, was ever pain,
  Was ever love, like thine?

Doxology.

Now let the Father, and the Son,
  And Spirit be adored,   [known,
Where there are works to make him
Or saints to love the Lord.

50 (131) C. M.   COWPER.

The Fountain.

THERE is a fountain filled with blood,
  Drawn from Immanuel's veins;
And sinners, plunged beneath that flood,
  Lose all their guilty stains.

2 The dying thief rejoiced to see
  That fountain in his day;
And there may I, though vile as he,
  Wash all my sins away.

3 Dear dying Lamb, thy precious blood
  Shall never lose its power,
Till all the ransomed Church of God
  Be saved to sin no more.

4 E'er since, by faith, I saw the stream
  Thy flowing wounds supply,
Redeeming love has been my theme,
  And shall be till I die.

5 Then in a nobler, sweeter song,
  I'll sing thy power to save,
When this poor lisping, stamm'ring
     tongue
Lies silent in the grave.

51 (134) 7s.

Rock of Ages.

ROCK of Ages, cleft for me,
   Let me hide myself in thee;
Let the water and the blood,
From thy wounded side which flowed,
Be of sin the double cure,
Save from wrath and make me pure.

2 Could my tears for ever flow,
Could my zeal no languor know,
These for sin could not atone;
Thou must save, and thou alone:
In my hand no price I bring,
Simply to thy cross I cling.

3 While I draw this fleeting breath,
When my eyes shall close in death,
When I rise to worlds unknown,
And behold thee on thy throne,
Rock of Ages, cleft for me,
Let me hide myself in thee.

52 (167) 8s, 7s, & 4.

Second Advent of Christ.

LO! he comes, with clouds descending,
   Once for favored sinners slain!
Thousand thousand saints, attending,
Swell the triumph of his train!
Hallelujah!
God appears on earth to reign.

2 Every eye shall now behold him
Robed in dreadful majesty;
Those who set at naught and sold him,
Pierced and nailed him to the tree,
Deeply wailing,
Shall the true Messiah see.

3 The dear tokens of his passion,
Still his dazzling body bears;
Cause of endless exultation
To his ransomed worshippers;
With what rapture
Gaze we on these glorious scars!

4 Yea, Amen! let all adore thee,
High on thy eternal throne,
Saviour, take the power and glory,
Claim the kingdom for thine own!
Jah! Jehovah!
Everlasting God, come down!

53 (154) 8s, 7s. BAKEWELL.

Priesthood of Christ. •

HAIL, thou once despised Jesus!
   Hail, thou Galilean King!
Thou didst suffer to release us;
Thou didst free salvation bring.
Hail, thou agonizing Saviour,
Bearer of our sin and shame!
By thy merits we find favor:
Life is given through thy name.

2 Paschal Lamb, by God appointed,
All our sins on thee were laid;
By almighty love anointed,
Thou hast full atonement made:
All thy people are forgiven,
Through the virtue of thy blood;
Opened is the gate of heaven;
Peace is made 'twixt man and God.

3 Jesus, hail! enthroned in glory,
There for ever to abide!
All the heavenly hosts adore thee,
Seated at thy Father's side:
There for sinners thou art pleading,
There thou dost our place prepare,
Ever for us interceding,
Till in glory we appear.

4 Worship, honor, power, and blessing,
Thou art worthy to receive:
Loudest praises, without ceasing,
Meet it is for us to give:
Help, ye bright angelic spirits,
Bring your sweetest, noblest lays:
Help to sing our Saviour's merits;
Help to chant Immanuel's praise.

NUREMBERG. 7s.

GERMAN.

54 (129) 7s. C. WESLEY.

"It is finished."

SONS of God, triumphant rise,
  Shout th' accomplished sacrifice!
Shout your sins in Christ forgiven,
Sons of God, and heirs of heaven!

2 Ye that round our altars throng,
  List'ning angels, join the song:
  Sing with us, ye heavenly powers,
  Pardon, grace, and glory, ours!

3 Love's mysterious work is done:
  Greet we now th' atoning Son:
  Healed and quickened by his blood,
  Joined to Christ, and one with God.

4 Him by faith we taste below,
  Mightier joys ordained to know,
  When his utmost grace we prove,
  Rise to heaven by perfect love.

3 *

55 (307) 7s. C. WESLEY.

Communion with Christ.

JESUS, all-redeeming Lord,
  Magnify thy dying word,
In thine ordinance appear,
Come and meet thy foll'wers here.

2 In the rite thou hast enjoined,
  Let us now our Saviour find;
  Drink thy blood for sinners shed,
  Taste thee in the broken bread.

3 Thou our faithful hearts prepare;
  Thou thy pard'ning grace declare;
  Thou that hast for sinners died,
  Show thyself the Crucified!

4 All the power of sin remove;
  Fill us with thy perfect love;
  Stamp us with the stamp divine;
  Seal our souls for ever thine.

56 (145) L. M.   WATTS.
Dying, rising, reigning.

HE dies! the Friend of sinners dies!
Lo! Salem's daughters weep
around;
A solemn darkness veils the skies;
A sudden trembling shakes the
ground:
Come, saints, and drop a tear or two
For him who groaned beneath your
load:
He shed a thousand drops for you,
A thousand drops of richer blood.

2 Here's love and grief beyond degree:
The Lord of glory dies for man!
But lo! what sudden joys we see!
Jesus, the dead, revives again!
The rising God forsakes the tomb;
Up to his Father's courts he flies;
Cherubic legions guard him home,
And shout him welcome to the skies!

3 Break off your tears, ye saints, and tell
How high your great Deliv'rer reigns;
Sing how he spoiled the hosts of hell,
And led the monster death in chains!
Say, "Live for ever, wondrous King!
Born to redeem, and strong to save!"
Then ask the monster, "Where's thy
sting?"
And, "Where's thy viet'ry, boasting
grave?"

57 (168) L. M.   C. WESLEY.
Rev. xi. 15.

HE comes! he comes! the Judge
severe!
The seventh trumpet speaks him near:
His lightnings flash, his thunders roll;
How welcome to the faithful soul!

2 From heaven angelic voices sound:
See the almighty Jesus crowned!
Girt with omnipotence and grace,
And glory decks the Saviour's face.

3 Descending on his azure throne,
He claims the kingdoms for his own:
The kingdoms all obey his word,
And hail him their triumphant Lord!

4 Shout, all the people of the sky,
And all the saints of the Most High:
Our Lord, who now his right obtains,
For ever and for ever reigns.

58 (180) S. M.   WATTS.
Psalm xlv. 1–7.

MY Saviour and my King,
Thy beauties are divine;
Thy lips with blessings overflow,
And every grace is thine.

2 Now make thy glories known,
Gird on thy dreadful sword,
And ride in majesty, to spread
The conquests of thy word.

3 Strike through thy stubborn foes,
Or melt their hearts t'obey;
While justice, meekness, grace, and
truth,
Attend thy glorious way.

59 (265) C. M.
The Minister's Theme.

JESUS, the name high over all
In hell, or earth, or sky!
Angels and men before it fall,
And devils fear and fly.

2 Jesus, the name to sinners dear,
The name to sinners given!
It scatters all their guilty fear;
It turns their hell to heaven.

3 Jesus the pris'ners' fetters breaks,
And bruises Satan's head;
Power into strengthless souls it speaks,
And life into the dead.

4 O that the world might taste and see
The riches of his grace!
The arms of love that compass me,
Would all mankind embrace!

5 His only righteousness I show,
His saving truth proclaim:
'Tis all my business here below
To cry "Behold the Lamb!"

6 Happy, if with my latest breath
I may but gasp his name:
Preach him to all, and cry in death,
"Behold, behold the Lamb!"

CORONATION. C. M. OLIVER HOLDEN.

60 (155) C. M. PERRONET.
Coronation of Christ.

ALL hail the power of Jesus' name!
 Let angels prostrate fall:
Bring forth the royal diadem,
 And crown him Lord of all.

2 Ye chosen seed of Israel's race,—
 A remnant weak and small,—
Hail him, who saves you by his grace,
 And crown him Lord of all.

3 Ye Gentile sinners, ne'er forget
 The wormwood and the gall:
Go, spread your trophies at his feet,
 And crown him Lord of all.

4 Let every kindred, every tribe
 On this terrestrial ball,
To him all majesty ascribe,
 And crown him Lord of all.

5 O that, with yonder sacred throng,
 We at his feet may fall!
We'll join the everlasting song,
 And crown him Lord of all.

61 (183) C. M. WATTS.
Rev. v. 11-13.

COME, let us join our cheerful songs
 With angels round the throne:
Ten thousand thousand are their tongues,
 But all their joys are one.

2 Worthy the Lamb that died, they cry,
 To be exalted thus:
Worthy the Lamb, our hearts reply,
 For he was slain for us.

3 Jesus is worthy to receive
 Honor and power Divine;
And blessings, more than we can give,
 Be, Lord, for ever thine.

4 The whole creation join in one
 To bless the sacred name
Of him that sits upon the throne,
 And to adore the Lamb.

Doxology.
Now let the Father, and the Son,
 And Spirit be adored, [known,
Where there are works to make him
 Or saints to love the Lord.

62 (158) 6s & 8s. C. WESLEY.
The Reign of Christ.

REJOICE, the Lord is King,
  Your Lord and King adore:
Mortals, give thanks, and sing,
  And triumph evermore:
Lift up your hearts, lift up your voice,
Rejoice, again I say, rejoice.

2 Jesus, the Saviour, reigns,
  The God of truth and love:
When he had purged our stains,
  He took his seat above:
Lift up your hearts, lift up your voice,
Rejoice, again I say, rejoice:

3 His kingdom cannot fail,
  He rules o'er earth and heaven;
The keys of death and hell
  Are to our Jesus given:
Lift up your hearts, lift up your voice,
Rejoice, again I say, rejoice.

4 He sits at God's right hand
  Till all his foes submit,
And bow to his command,
  And fall beneath his feet:
Lift up your hearts, lift up your voice,
Rejoice, again I say, rejoice.

5 He all his foes shall quell,
  Shall all our sins destroy;
And every bosom swell
  With pure seraphic joy:
Lift up your hearts, lift up your voice,
Rejoice, again I say, rejoice.

63 (177) 6s & 8s. C. WESLEY.
The Saviour's Praise.

LET earth and heaven agree,
  Angels and men be joined,
To celebrate with me
  The Saviour of mankind;
T' adore the all-atoning Lamb,
And bless the sound of Jesus' name.

2 Jesus! transporting sound!
  The joy of earth and heaven:
No other help is found,
  No other name is given,
By which we can salvation have;
But Jesus came the world to save.

3 Jesus! harmonious name!
  It charms the hosts above;
They evermore proclaim,
  And wonder at his love!
'T is all their happiness to gaze,
'T is heaven to see our Jesus' face.

4 His name the sinner hears,
  And is from sin set free;
'T is music in his ears;
  'T is life and victory:
New songs do now his lips employ,
And dances his glad heart for joy.

5 Stung by the scorpion, sin,
  My poor expiring soul
The balmy sound drinks in,
  And is at once made whole:
See there my Lord upon the tree!
I hear, I feel he died for me.

6 O unexampled love!
  O all-redeeming grace!
How swiftly didst thou move
  To save a fallen race!
What shall I do to make it known
What thou for all mankind hast done?

7 O for a trumpet voice,
  On all the world to call!
To bid their hearts rejoice
  In him who died for all!
For all my Lord was crucified;
For all, for all my Saviour died.

64 (633) 6s & 8s.
"Leaving us an example."

SEE where our great High Priest
  Before the Lord appears,
And on his loving breast
  The tribes of Israel bears,
Never without his people seen,
The Head of all believing men!

2 With him the corner-stone
  The living stones conjoin,
Christ and his Church are one,
  One body and one vine;
For us he uses all his powers,
And all he has, or is, is ours.

ARLINGTON. C. M.

Moderato.

65 (160) C. M.   BEDDOME.
" Let all the angels of God worship him.".

HOW great the wisdom, power, and
  grace
Which in redemption shine!
The heavenly host with joy confess
The work is all divine.

2 Before his feet they cast their crowns,—
Those crowns which Jesus gave,—
And, with ten thousand thousand tongues,
Proclaim his power to save.

3 They tell the triumphs of his cross,
The suff'rings which he bore,—
How low he stooped, how high he rose,
And rose to stoop no more.

4 O let them still their voices raise,
And still their songs renew:
Salvation well deserves the praise
Of men and angels too!

66 (186) C. M.   WATTS.
Salvation.

SALVATION, O the joyful sound!
  'T is pleasure to our ears:
A sov'reign balm for every wound,
A cordial for our fears.

2 Buried in sorrow and in sin,
At hell's dark door we lay;

But we arise by grace divine,
To see a heavenly day.

3 Salvation! let the echo fly
The spacious earth around,
While all the armies of the sky
Conspire to raise the sound.

67 (188) C. M.   WATTS.
Stupendous Love.

PLUNGED in a gulf of dark despair,
  We wretched sinners lay,
Without one cheering beam of hope,
Or spark of glimm'ring day.

2 With pitying eyes the Prince of grace
Beheld our helpless grief:
He saw, and (O amazing love!)
He ran to our relief.

3 Down from the shining seats above
With joyful haste he fled,
Entered the grave in mortal flesh,
And dwelt among the dead.

4 O for this love let rocks and hills
Their lasting silence break!
And all harmonious human tongues
The Saviour's praises speak.

5 Angels, assist our mighty joys,
Strike all your harps of gold;
But when you raise your highest notes,
His love can ne'er be told!

C

PORTUGAL. L. M.

THORLEY.

68 (189) L. M.

[From the Latin of St. Bernard.]

Love which passeth Knowledge.

O F him who did salvation bring,
   I could for ever think and sing:
Arise, ye needy, he'll relieve;
Arise, ye guilty, he'll forgive.

2 Ask but his grace, and lo, 'tis given!
  Ask, and he turns your hell to heaven:
Though sin and sorrow wound my soul,
Jesus, thy balm will make it whole.

3 To shame our sins he blushed in blood,
  He closed his eyes to show us God:
Let all the world fall down and know
That none but God such love can show.

4 'Tis thee I love, for thee alone
  I shed my tears and make my moan!
Where'er I am, where'er I move,
I meet the object of my love.

5 Insatiate to this spring I fly:
  I drink, and yet am ever dry:
Ah! who against thy charms is proof?
Ah! who that loves can love enough?

69 (184) L. M.

WATTS.

Rev. v. 12–14.

W HAT equal honors shall we bring
   To thee, O Lord our God, the
     Lamb,
When all the notes that angels sing
Are far inferior to thy name?

2 Worthy is he that once was slain,
  The Prince of life, that groaned and
    died;
Worthy to rise, and live, and reign
At his almighty Father's side.

3 Power and dominion are his due
  Who stood condemned at Pilate's bar:
Wisdom belongs to Jesus too,
  Though he was charged with madness
    here.

4 All riches are his native right,
  Yet he sustained amazing loss:
To him ascribe eternal might,
Who left his weakness on the cross.

5 Blessings for ever on the Lamb,
  Who bore our sin, and curse, and pain:
Let angels sound his sacred name,
  And every creature say, Amen!

70 **(622)** S. M.   HAMMOND.

"Sing praises to God."

AWAKE, and sing the song
Of Moses and the Lamb;
Tune every heart and every tongue,
To praise the Saviour's name.

2 Sing of his dying love;
Sing of his rising power;
Sing how he intercedes above
For those whose sins he bore.

3 Tell, in seraphic strains,
What he has done for you;
How he has taken off your chains,
And form'd your hearts anew.

4 His faithfulness proclaim
While life to you is given;
Join hands and hearts to praise his name,
Till we all meet in heaven.

71 **(196)** C. M.

The Name of Jesus.

HOW sweet the name of Jesus sounds
In a believer's ear!
It soothes his sorrows, heals his wounds,
And drives away his fear.

2 It makes the wounded spirit whole,
And calms the troubled breast;
'T is manna to the hungry soul,
And to the weary, rest.

3 Dear Name, the rock on which I build,
My shield and hiding place;
My never-failing treasury, fill'd
With boundless stores of grace.

4 Jesus, my Shepherd, Husband, Friend,
My Prophet, Priest, and King!
My Lord, my Life, my Way, my End,
Accept the praise I bring.

5 Weak is the effort of my heart,
And cold my warmest thought;
But when I see thee as thou art,
I'll praise thee as I ought.

6 Till then I would thy love proclaim
With every fleeting breath;
And may the music of thy name
Refresh my soul in death.

72 **(631)** C. M.   C. WESLEY.

"I have chosen thee in the furnace."

THEE, Jesus, full of truth and grace,
Thee, Saviour, we adore:
Thee in affliction's furnace praise,
And magnify thy power.

2 Thy power, in human weakness shown,
Shall make us all entire:
We now thy guardian presence own,
And walk unburned in fire.

3 Thee, Son of man, by faith we see,
And glory in our guide;
Surrounded and upheld by thee,
The fiery test abide.

4 The fire our graces shall refine,
Till, moulded from above,
We bear the character divine,
The stamp of perfect love.

73 **(862)** L. M.   H. K. WHITE.

Star of Bethlehem.

WHEN, marshalled on the nightly
plain,
The glitt'ring host bestud the sky,
One star alone of all the train
Can fix the sinner's wand'ring eye.
Hark! hark! to God the chorus breaks,
From every host, from every gem;
But one alone the Saviour speaks,
It is the Star of Bethlehem.

2 Once on the raging seas I rode;
The storm was loud, the night was
dark,
The ocean yawned, and rudely blowed
The wind, that tossed my found'ring
bark.
Deep horror then my vitals froze;
Death-struck, I ceased the tide to
stem;
When suddenly a star arose,
It was the Star of Bethlehem.

3 It was my guide, my light, my all;
It bade my dark foreboding cease;
And, through the storm and danger's
thrall,
It led me to the port of peace.
Now, safely moored, my perils o'er,
I'll sing, first in night's diadem,
For ever, and for evermore,
The Star! — the Star of Bethlehem!

THATCHER. S. M.

74 (120) S. M.   DODDRIDGE.
Attraction of the Cross.

BEHOLD th' amazing sight,
    The Saviour lifted high:
Behold the Son of God's delight
Expire in agony.

2 For whom, for whom, my heart,
    Were all these sorrows borne?
Why did he feel that piercing smart,
    And meet that various scorn?

3 For love of us he bled,
    And all in torture died:
'T was love that bowed his fainting head,
    And ope'd his gushing side.

4 I see, and I adore
    In sympathy of love:
I feel the strong, attractive power,
    To lift my soul above.

75 (111) S. M.   BEDDOME.
"He beheld the City, and wept over it."

DID Christ o'er sinners weep,
    And shall our cheeks be dry?
Let floods of penitential grief
Burst forth from every eye.

2 The Son of God in tears
    The wond'ring angels see;

Be thou astonished, O my soul:
He shed those tears for thee.

3 He wept that we might weep;
    Each sin demands a tear:
In heaven alone no sin is found,
And there's no weeping there.

76 (166) S. M.   C. WESLEY.
Christ our Advocate.

REDEEMER of mankind,
    Who on thy name rely,
A constant intercourse we find
Opened 'twixt earth and sky.

2 Mercy, and grace, and peace,
    Descend through thee alone;
And thou dost all our services
    Present before the throne.

3 On us thy Father's love
    Is for thy sake bestowed:
Thou art our Advocate above,
    Thou art our way to God:

4 Our way to God we trace,
    And through thy name forgiven,
From step to step, from grace to grace,
On thee we climb to heaven.

77 (185) 7s.
Redeeming Love.

NOW begin the heavenly theme;
  Sing aloud in Jesus' name:
Ye who his salvation prove,
Triumph in redeeming love.

2 Ye who see the Father's grace
Beaming on the Saviour's face,
As to Canaan on ye move,
Praise and bless redeeming love.

3 Mourning souls, dry up your tears;
Banish all your guilty fears;
See your guilt and curse remove,
Cancelled by redeeming love.

4 Welcome all by sin opprest,
Welcome to his sacred rest:
Nothing brought him from above,—
Nothing but redeeming love.

5 Hither, then, your music bring;
Strike aloud each cheerful string;
Mortals, join the hosts above,—
Join to praise redeeming love.

78 (187) C. M. S. STENNETT.
Indebtedness to Christ.

MAJESTIC sweetness sits enthroned
  Upon the Saviour's brow:
His head with radiant glories crowned,
His lips with grace o'erflow.

2 He saw me plunged in deep distress,
And flew to my relief:
For me he bore the shameful cross,
And carried all my grief.

3 To heaven, the place of his abode,
He brings my weary feet,
Shows me the glories of my God,
And makes my joy complete.

4 Since from his bounty I receive
Such proofs of love divine,
Had I a thousand hearts to give,
Lord, they should all be thine.

4

79 (603) C. M.
Relieving Christ in his Members.

JESUS, my Lord, how rich thy grace!
  Thy bounties, how complete!
How shall I count the matchless sum?
How pay the mighty debt?

2 High on a throne of radiant light
Dost thou exalted shine;
What can my poverty bestow,
When all the worlds are thine?

3 But thou hast brethren here below,
The partners of thy grace,
And wilt confess their humble names
Before thy Father's face.

4 In them thou may'st be clothed and fed,
And visited and cheered,
And in their accents of distress
My Saviour's voice is heard.

5 Thy face with rev'rence and with love,
I in thy poor would see;
O rather let me beg my bread,
Than hold it back from thee!

80 (153) C. M. WATTS.
Heb. iv. 14-16.

WITH joy we meditate the grace
  Of our High Priest above:
His heart is made of tenderness,
His bowels melt with love.

2 Touched with a sympathy within,
He knows our feeble frame:
He knows what sore temptations mean,
For he hath felt the same.

3 He in the days of feeble flesh
Poured out strong cries and tears;
And in his measure feels afresh
What every member bears.

4 He 'll never quench the smoking flax,
But raise it to a flame:
The bruised reed he never breaks,
Nor scorns the meanest name.

5 Then let our humble faith address
His mercy and his power:
We shall obtain deliv'ring grace
In the distressing hour.

TALLIS' HYMN. L. M.   TALLIS.

81 (193) L. M.   WATTS.
Wonders of the Cross.

NATURE with open volume stands
　　To spread her Maker's praise
　　　　abroad,
And every labor of his hands
　　Shows something worthy of a God.

2 But in the grace that rescued man
　　His brightest form of glory shines:
Here, on the cross, 't is fairest drawn
　　In precious blood and crimson lines.

3 O! the sweet wonders of that cross,
　　Where God, the Saviour, loved and
　　　　died!
Her noblest life my spirit draws
　　From his dear wounds and bleeding
　　　　side.

4 I would for ever speak his name,
　　In sounds to mortal ears unknown;
With angels join to praise the Lamb,
　　And worship at his Father's throne.

82 (38) L. M.   C. WESLEY.
The Father of Mercies.

GOD of my life, whose gracious power
　　Through various deaths my soul
　　　　hath led,
Or turned aside the fatal hour,
　　Or lifted up my sinking head!

2 In all my ways thy hand I own,
　　Thy ruling providence I see:
Assist me still my course to run,
　　And still direct my paths to thee.

3 Whither, O whither should I fly,
　　But to my loving Saviour's breast?
Secure within thine arms to lie,
　　And safe beneath thy wings to rest.

4 I have no skill the snare to shun,
　　But thou, O Christ, my wisdom art!
I ever into ruin run,
　　But thou art greater than my heart.

5 Foolish, and impotent, and blind,
　　Lead me a way I have not known:
Bring me where I my heaven may find,
　　The heaven of loving thee alone.

SHIRLAND. S. M.
STANLEY.

83 **(206)** S. M. MONTGOMERY.
Pentecost.

LORD God, the Holy Ghost,
    In this accepted hour,
As on the day of Pentecost,
Descend in all thy power!

2 We meet with one accord
    In our appointed place,
And wait the promise of our Lord,
The Spirit of all grace.

3 Like mighty rushing wind
    Upon the waves beneath,
Move with one impulse every mind,
One soul, one feeling, breathe.

4 The young, the old, inspire
    With wisdom from above;
And give us hearts and tongues of fire
To pray, and praise, and love.

84 **(212)** S. M. C. WESLEY.
Spirit of Faith.

SPIRIT of faith, come down,
    Reveal the things of God;
And make to us the Godhead known,
And witness with the blood:

'T is thine the blood t' apply,
    And give us eyes to see
Who did for every sinner die,
Hath surely died for me.

2 No man can truly say
    That Jesus is the Lord,
Unless thou take the veil away,
    And breathe the living word:
Then, only then, we feel
    Our int'rest in his blood;
And cry, with joy unspeakable,
    "Thou art my Lord, my God!"

85 **(220)** S. M. BEDDOME.
Holy Spirit's Influences Sought.

COME, Holy Spirit, come,
    With energy divine,
And on this poor, benighted soul,
    With beams of mercy shine.

2 O melt this frozen heart;
    This stubborn will subdue;
Each evil passion overcome,
    And form me all anew!

3 The profit will be mine,
    But thine shall be the praise:
And unto thee will I devote
The remnant of my days.

86 (213) C. M. WATTS.
Witness and Seal.

WHY should the children of a King
Go mourning all their days?
Great Comforter, descend, and bring
The tokens of thy grace.

2 Dost thou not dwell in all thy saints,
And seal the heirs of heaven?
When wilt thou banish my complaints,
And show my sins forgiven?

3 Assure my conscience of her part
In the Redeemer's blood;
And bear thy witness with my heart,
That I am born of God.

4 Thou art the earnest of his love,
The pledge of joys to come:
May thy blest wings, celestial Dove,
Safely convey me home!

87 (214) C. M. DODDRIDGE.
Witness of Adoption.

SOVEREIGN of all the worlds on high,
Allow my humble claim;
Nor, while a worm would raise its head,
Disdain a Father's name.

2 "My Father, God!" how sweet the
sound!
How tender and how dear!
Not all the melody of heaven
Could so delight the ear.

3 Come, sacred Spirit, seal the name
On my expanding heart;
And show that in Jehovah's grace
I share a filial part.

4 Cheered by a signal so divine,
Unwav'ring I believe:
Thou know'st I "Abba, Father," cry;
Nor can the sign deceive.

Doxology.

Now let the Father, and the Son,
And Spirit be adored, [known,
Where there are works to make him.
Or saints to love the Lord.

88 (222) C. M. BEDDOME.
Invoked.

CELESTIAL Dove, Come from above,
And guide me in thy ways:
My heart prepare For solemn prayer,
And tune my lips to praise.

2 Open mine eyes, And make me wise,
My int'rest to discern:
From every sin, Without, within,
Incline my heart to turn.

3 Fly to my aid, When I'm afraid,
Or plunged in deep distress;
My foes subdue, And bring me through
This howling wilderness.

89 (224) L. M. C. WESLEY.
His Departure earnestly Deprecated.

STAY, thou insulted Spirit, stay!
Though I have done thee such de-
spite;
Nor cast the sinner quite away,
Nor take thine everlasting flight.

2 Though I have steeled my stubborn
heart,
And still shook off my guilty fears;
And vexed, and urged thee to depart,
For many long rebellious years:

3 Though I have most unfaithful been
Of all who e'er thy grace received;
Ten thousand times thy goodness seen,
Ten thousand times thy goodness
grieved.

4 Yet O! the chief of sinners spare,
In honor of my great High Priest;
Nor in thy righteous anger swear
T' exclude me from thy people's rest.

5 This only woe I deprecate;
This only plague I pray remove;
Nor leave me in my lost estate;
Nor curse me with this want of love.

6 Now, Lord, my weary soul release,
Upraise me with thy gracious hand,
And guide me into perfect peace,
And bring me to the promised land.

DUNDEE. C. M.

90 **(209)** C. M.　　C. WESLEY.

The Interpreter.

COME, Holy Ghost, our hearts inspire,
　Let us thine influence prove:
Source of the old prophetic fire,
　Fountain of life and love.

2 Come, Holy Ghost — for, moved by thee,
　The prophets wrote and spoke —
Unlock the truth, thyself the key:
　Unseal the sacred book.

3 Expand thy wings, celestial Dove,
　Brood o'er our nature's night;
On our disordered spirits move,
　And let there now be light.

4 God, through himself, we then shall
　know,
If thou within us shine:
And sound, with all thy saints below,
　The depths of love divine.
　4 *

91 **(221)** C. M.　　WATTS.

His Quickenings Implored.

COME, Holy Spirit, heavenly Dove,
　With all thy quick'ning powers,
Kindle a flame of sacred love
　In these cold hearts of ours.

2 Look how we grovel here below,
　Fond of these earthly toys;
Our souls, how heavily they go,
　To reach eternal joys!

3 In vain we tune our formal songs,
　In vain we strive to rise;
Hosannas languish on our tongues,
　And our devotion dies.

4 And shall we then for ever live
　At this poor dying rate?
Our love so faint, so cold to thee,
　And thine to us so great?

92 (325) 6s & 8s.   C. WESLEY.

The Year of Jubilee.

BLOW ye the trumpet, blow,
    The gladly solemn sound;
Let all the nations know,
    To earth's remotest bound,
The year of jubilee is come;
Return, ye ransomed sinners, home.

2 Jesus, our great High Priest,
    Hath full atonement made:
Ye weary spirits, rest;
    Ye mournful souls, be glad:
The year of jubilee is come;
Return, ye ransomed sinners, home.

3 Extol the Lamb of God,
    The all-atoning Lamb;
Redemption through his blood
Throughout the world proclaim:
The year of jubilee is come;
Return, ye ransomed sinners, home.

4 Ye slaves of sin and hell,
    Your liberty receive,
And safe in Jesus dwell,
    And blessed in Jesus live:
The year of jubilee is come;
Return, ye ransomed sinners, home.

5 Ye who have sold for naught
    Your heritage above,
Receive it back unbought,
    The gift of Jesus' love:
The year of jubilee is come;
Return, ye ransomed sinners, home.

6 The gospel trumpet hear,
    The news of heavenly grace;

And, saved from earth, appear
    Before your Saviour's face;
The year of jubilee is come;
Return, ye ransomed sinners, home.

93 (333) C. M.   WATTS.

Isaiah lv. 1–3.

LET every mortal ear attend,
    And every heart rejoice;
The trumpet of the gospel sounds
    With an inviting voice.

2 Ho! all ye hungry, starving souls,
    That feed upon the wind,
And vainly strive with earthly toys
    To fill an empty mind;

3 Eternal Wisdom hath prepared
    A soul-reviving feast,
And bids your longing appetites
    The rich provision taste.

4 Ho! ye that pant for living streams,
    And pine away and die,
Here you may quench your raging thirst
    With springs that never dry.

5 Rivers of love and mercy here,
    In a rich ocean join:
Salvation, in abundance, flows
    Like floods of milk and wine.

6 The happy gates of gospel grace
    Stand open night and day:
Lord, we are come to seek supplies,
    And drive our wants away.

NETTLETON. 8s & 7s. (Double.)

94 (330) 8s, 7s & 4. HART.

The Invitation.

COME, ye sinners, poor and needy,
  Weak and wounded, sick and sore,
Jesus ready stands to save you,
  Full of pity, love, and power :
    He is able,
  He is willing, doubt no more.

2 Now, ye needy, come and welcome,
    God's free bounty glorify :
  True belief and true repentance,
    Every grace that brings you nigh,
      Without money,
    Come to Jesus Christ and buy.

3 Let not conscience make you linger :
    Nor of fitness fondly dream :
  All the fitness he requireth
    Is to feel your need of him :
      This he gives you,
    'T is the Spirit's glimm'ring beam.

4 Come, ye weary, heavy-laden,
    Bruised and mangled by the fall,

If you tarry till you 're better,
    You will never come at all :
  Not the righteous,
    Sinners Jesus came to call.

5 Agonizing in the garden,
    Lo! your Maker prostrate lies !
  On the bloody tree behold him !
    Hear him cry before he dies,
      " It is finished !"
    Sinners, will not this suffice?

6 Lo! th' incarnate God ascending,
    Pleads the merit of his blood ;
  Venture on him, venture freely,
    Let no other trust intrude :
      None but Jesus
    Can do helpless sinners good.

7 Saints and angels, joined in concert,
    Sing the praises of the Lamb,
  While the blissful seats of heaven
    Sweetly echo with his name :
      Hallelujah !
    Sinners here may do the same.

95 (327) L. M.

The Invitation.

COME, O ye sinners, to your Lord,
  In Christ to paradise restored;
His proffer'd benefits embrace,
The plenitude of gospel grace:

2 A pardon written with his blood,
  The favor and the peace of God;
  The seeing eye, the feeling sense,
  The mystic joys of penitence:

3 The godly fear, the pleasing smart,
  The meltings of a broken heart;
  The tears that tell your sins forgiven;
  The sighs that waft your souls to Heaven.

4 The guiltless shame, the sweet distress,
  Th' unutterable tenderness;
  The genuine, meek humility;
  The wonder, "Why such love to me!"

5 Th' o'erwhelming power of saving grace,
  The sight that veils the seraph's face;
  The speechless awe that dares not move,
  And all the silent heaven of love.

96 (331) L. M.   C. WESLEY.

Isaiah lv. 1–3.

HO! every one that thirsts, draw nigh;
  'T is God invites the fallen race:
Mercy and free salvation buy;
Buy wine, and milk, and gospel grace.

2 Come to the living waters, come!
  Sinners, obey your Maker's call:
  Return, ye weary wand'rers, home,
  And find my grace is free for all.

3 See from the rock a fountain rise;
  For you in healing streams it rolls;
  Money ye need not bring, nor price,
  Ye lab'ring, burdened, sin-sick souls.

4 Nothing ye in exchange shall give,
  Leave all you have, and are, behind;
  Frankly the gift of God receive,
  Pardon and peace in Jesus find.

97 (335) C. M.   C. WESLEY.

The Chief of Sinners Invited.

LOVERS of pleasure more than God,
  For you he suffered pain:
Swearers, for you he spilt his blood;
And shall he bleed in vain?

2 Misers, his life for you he paid,
  Your basest crimes he bore;
  Drunkards, your sins on him were laid,
  That you might sin no more.

3 The God of love, to earth he came,
  That you might come to heaven:
  Believe, believe in Jesus' name,
  And all your sin 's forgiven.

4 Believe in him who died for thee,
  And sure as he hath died,
  Thy debt is paid, thy soul is free,
  And thou art justified.

98 (350) C. M.   C. WESLEY.

Rev. iii. 20.

COME, let us who in Christ believe,
  Our common Saviour praise:
To him, with joyful voices, give
The glory of his grace.

2 He now stands knocking at the door
  Of every sinner's heart:
  The worst need keep him out no more,
  Or force him to depart.

3 Through grace we hearken to thy voice,
  Yield to be saved from sin;
  In sure and certain hope rejoice,
  That thou wilt enter in.

4 Come quickly in, thou heavenly Guest,
  Nor ever hence remove:
  But sup with us, and let the feast
  Be everlasting love.

ROTHWELL. L. M.

99 (326) L. M.   C. WESLEY.
The Gospel Supper.

SINNERS, obey the gospel word!
Haste to the supper of my Lord:
Be wise to know your gracious day;
All things are ready; come away.

2 Ready the Father is to own
And kiss his late-returning son:
Ready your loving Saviour stands,
And spreads for you his bleeding hands.

3 Ready the Spirit of his love
Just now your hardness to remove;
T' apply and witness with the blood,
And wash and seal the sons of God.

4 Ready for you the angels wait,
To triumph in your blessed estate:
Tuning their harps, they long to praise
The wonders of redeeming grace.

5 The Father, Son, and Holy Ghost,
Are ready with their shining host:
All heaven is ready to resound,
"The dead 's alive! the lost is found!"

100 (328) L. M.   C. WESLEY.
The Hearty Welcome.

COME, sinners, to the gospel feast;
Let every soul be Jesus' guest:
Ye need not one be left behind,
For God hath bidden all mankind.

2 Sent by my Lord, on you I call;
The invitation is to all:
Come, all the world! come, sinner, thou;
All things in Christ are ready now.

3 Come, all ye souls by sin oppressed,
Ye restless wand'rers after rest, [blind,
Ye poor, and maimed, and halt, and
In Christ a hearty welcome find.

4 My message as from God receive:
Ye all may come to Christ and live:
O let his love your hearts constrain,
Nor suffer him to die in vain!

101 (329) C. M.

And yet there is Room.

YE wretched, hungry, starving poor,
    Behold a royal feast!
Where mercy spreads her bounteous
    store
For every humble guest.

2 See, Jesus stands with open arms;
  He calls, he bids you come:
  O stay not back, though fear alarms!
  For yet there still is room.

3 O come, and with his children taste
  The blessings of his love;
  While hope attends the sweet repast
  Of nobler joys above!

102 (334) C. M.   E. JONES.

Come to Jesus.

COME, humble sinner, in whose breast
    A thousand thoughts revolve, —
Come, with your guilt and fear oppressed,
And make this last resolve:

2 I 'll go to Jesus, though my sin
  Hath like a mountain rose;
  I know his courts, I 'll enter in,
  Whatever may oppose:

3 Prostrate I 'll lie before his throne,
  And there my guilt confess;
  I 'll tell him I 'm a wretch undone,
  Without his sovereign grace:

4 I 'll to the gracious King approach,
  Whose sceptre pardon gives;
  Perhaps he may command my touch,
  And then the suppliant lives.

5 Perhaps he may admit my plea,
  Perhaps will hear my prayer;
  But if I perish, I will pray,
  And perish only there.

6 I can but perish if I go,
  I am resolved to try;
  For if I stay away I know
  I must for ever die.

7 But if I die with mercy sought,
  When I the King have tried,
  This were to die (delightful thought!)
  As sinner never died.

103 (340) C. M.

The Free Invitation.

THE Saviour calls — let every ear
    Attend the heavenly sound;
Ye doubting souls, dismiss your fear,
Hope smiles reviving round.

2 For every thirsty. longing heart,
  Here streams of bounty flow;
  And life, and health, and bliss, impart
  To banish mortal woe.

3 Ye sinners, come; 't is mercy's voice,
  The gracious call obey:
  Mercy invites to heavenly joys —
  And can you yet delay?

4 Dear Saviour, draw reluctant hearts!
  To thee let sinners fly,
  And take the bliss thy love imparts;
  And drink, and never die.

104 (341) C. M.

The Free Invitation.

JESUS, thy blessings are not few,
    Nor is thy gospel weak:
Thy grace can melt the stubborn Jew,
And bow th' aspiring Greek.

2 Wide as the reach of Satan's rage
  Doth thy salvation flow;
  'T is not confined to sex or age,
  The lofty or the low.

3 While grace is offer'd to the prince,
  The poor may take their share;
  No mortal has a just pretence
  To perish in despair.

4 Come, all ye vilest sinners, come;
  He 'll form your souls anew;
  His gospel and his heart have room
  For rebels such as you.

MEAR. C. M.

111 (348) C. M.
Worth of the Soul.

WHAT is the thing of greatest price,
The whole creation round?
That which was lost in Paradise,
That which in Christ is found:

2 The soul of man — Jehovah's breath —
That keeps two worlds at strife;
Hell moves beneath to work its death,
Heaven stoops to give it life.

3 God, to reclaim it, did not spare
His well-beloved Son;
Jesus, to save it, deign'd to bear
The sins of all in one.

4 The Holy Spirit seal'd the plan,
And pledged the blood divine,
To ransom every soul of man; —
That price was paid for mine.

5 And is this treasure borne below,
In earthen vessels frail?
Can none its utmost value know,
Till flesh and spirit fail?

6 Then let us gather round the cross,
That knowledge to obtain;
Not by the soul's eternal loss,
But everlasting gain.

112 (353) C. M.
Urgent Appeal.

SINNERS, the voice of God regard,
'T is mercy speaks to-day;
He calls you by his sacred word
From sin's destructive way.

2 Like the rough sea that cannot rest,
You live devoid of peace;
A thousand stings within your breast
Deprive your souls of ease.

3 Your way is dark, and leads to hell;
Why will you persevere?
Can you in endless torments dwell,
Shut up in black despair?

4 Why will you in the crooked ways
Of sin and folly go?
In pain you travel all your days,
To reap eternal woe.

5 But he that turns to God shall live
Through his abounding grace;
His mercy will the guilt forgive
Of those that seek his face.

6 Bow to the sceptre of his word,
Renouncing every sin;
Submit to him, your sovereign Lord,
And learn his will divine.

113 (352) 11s & 10s.

Consolation for the Penitent.

COME, ye disconsolate, where'er you languish,
Come, and at God's altar fervently kneel;
Here bring your wounded hearts, here tell your anguish;
Earth has no sorrow that Heaven cannot heal.

2 Joy of the desolate, Light of the straying,
Hope of the penitent, fadeless and pure;
Here speaks the Comforter, in God's name saying,
Earth has no sorrow that Heaven cannot cure.

3 Go, ask the infidel what boon he brings us, —
What charm for aching hearts he can reveal,
Sweet as the heavenly promise hope sings us,
Earth has no sorrow that God cannot heal.

114 (344) 7s. C. WESLEY.

Fly to Jesus.

WEARY souls that wander wide
From the central point of bliss,
Turn to Jesus crucified,
Fly to those dear wounds of his;
Sink into the purple flood;
Rise into the life of God.

2 Find in Christ the way of peace,
Peace unspeakable, unknown!
By his pain he gives you ease,
Life by his expiring groan;
Rise exalted by his fall,
Find in Christ your all in all.

3 O believe the record true,
God to you his Son hath given;
Ye may now be happy too;
Find on earth the light of heaven:
Live the life of heaven above,
All the life of glorious love.

4 This the universal bliss,
Bliss for every soul designed;
God's primeval promise this,
God's great gift to all mankind.

Blessed in Christ this moment be,
Blessed to all eternity!

115 (349) L. M.

The Stranger at the Door.

BEHOLD a stranger at the door,
He gently knocks, has knock'd before,
Has waited long, is waiting still,
You use no other friend so ill.

2 But will he prove a friend indeed?
He will — the very friend you need;
The man of Nazareth is he,
With garments died, from Calvary.

3 O lovely attitude! he stands
With melting heart and open hands,
O matchless kindness! and he shows
That matchless kindness to his foes.

4 Rise, touch'd with gratitude divine;
Turn out his enemy and thine,
Turn out that hateful monster, sin,
And let the heavenly stranger in.

116 (385) 7s. C. WESLEY.

The Invitation Accepted.

COME, ye weary sinners, come,
All who groan beneath your load;
Jesus calls his wand'rers home:
Hasten to your pard'ning God.
Come, ye guilty souls, oppressed,
Answer to the Saviour's call, —
"Come, and I will give you rest:
Come, and I will save you all."

2 Jesus, full of truth and love,
We thy kindest word obey;
Faithful let thy mercies prove,
Take our load of guilt away:
Fain we would on thee rely,
Cast on thee our every care,
To thine arms of mercy fly,
Find our lasting quiet there.

3 Burdened with a world of grief,
Burdened with our sinful load,
Burdened with this unbelief,
Burdened with the wrath of God;
Lo! we come to thee for ease,
True and gracious as thou art;
Now our groaning souls release,
Write forgiveness on our heart.

WINDHAM. L. M.

117 (354) L. M.   DWIGHT.
" Now is the Accepted Time."

WHILE life prolongs its precious light,
  Mercy is found, and peace is given;
But soon, ah soon, approaching night
Shall blot out every hope of heaven.

2 While God invites, how blessed the day!
  How sweet the gospel's charming
    sound!
Come, sinners, haste, O haste away,
While yet a pard'ning God is found.

3 Soon, borne on time's most rapid wing,
  Shall death command you to the grave,
Before his bar your spirits bring,
And none be found to hear or save.

4 In that lone land of deep despair
  No Sabbath's heavenly light shall rise,
No God regard your bitter prayer,
 No Saviour call you to the skies.

118 (693) L. M.   W. SCOTT.
Dies iræ.

THE day of wrath, that dreadful day,
  When heaven and earth shall pass
    away!
What power shall be the sinner's stay?
How shall he meet that dreadful day —

2 When, shriv'ling like a parched scroll,
  The flaming heavens together roll;

And, louder yet, and yet more dread,
Swells the high trump that wakes the
    dead?

3 O on that day, that wrathful day,
  When man to judgment wakes from clay,
Be thou, O Christ, the sinner's stay,
Though heaven and earth shall pass
  away!

119 (351) L. M.   COLLYER.
" Return unto me."

RETURN, O wanderer, return!
  And seek an injured Father's face;
Those warm desires that in thee burn
Were kindled by reclaiming grace.

2 Return, O wanderer, return,
  And seek a Father's melting heart;
His pitying eyes thy grief discern,
His hand shall heal thine inward smart.

3 Return, O wanderer, return,
  Thy Saviour bids thy spirit live;
Go to his bleeding feet, and learn
How freely Jesus can forgive.

4 Return, O wanderer, return,
  And wipe away the falling tear;
'T is God who says, "No longer mourn;"
'T is mercy's voice invites thee near.

120 **(357)** C. M.

Acts xvii. 30, 31.

REPENT, the voice celestial cries,
  No longer dare delay;
The wretch that scorns the mandate
  dies, —
And meets a fiery day.

2 The summons goes through all the earth,
  Let earth attend and fear;
Listen, ye men of royal birth,
  And let your vassals hear.

3 Together in his presence bow,
  And all your guilt confess;
Accept the offered Saviour now,
  Nor trifle with the grace.

4 Bow, ere the awful trumpet sound,
  And call you to his bar;
For mercy knows th' appointed bound,
  And turns to vengeance there.

121 **(358)** C. M.

Romans ii. 4, 5.

UNGRATEFUL sinners, whence this
  scorn
Of long-extended grace?
And whence this madness, that insults
Th' Almighty to his face?

2 Is it because his patience waits,
  And pitying bowels move,
You multiply audacious crimes,
  And spurn his richest love?

3 Is all the treasured wrath so small,
  You labor still for more,
Though not eternal rolling years
  Can e'er exhaust the store?

4 Swift doth the day of vengeance come,
  Which must your sentence seal;
And righteous judgment, now unknown,
  In all its pomp reveal.

5 Alarmed and melted at thy voice,
  Our conquered hearts would bow;
And to escape the Thunderer then,
  Embrace the Saviour now.

122 **(360)** 7s.   T. Scott.

"Escape for thy life."

HASTEN, sinner, to be wise;
  Stay not for the morrow's sun;
Wisdom, if thou still despise,
  Harder is she to be won.

2 Hasten, mercy to implore;
  Stay not for the morrow's sun;
Lest thy season should be o'er
  Ere this evening's stage be run.

3 Hasten, sinner, to return;
  Stay not for the morrow's sun;
Lest thy lamp should cease to burn
  Ere salvation's work is done.

4 Hasten, sinner, to be blest;
  Stay not for the morrow's sun;
Lest the curse should thee arrest
  Ere the morrow is begun.

123   L. M.   Stowell.

The Mercy-Seat.

FROM every stormy wind that blows,
  From every swelling tide of woes,
There is a calm, a sure retreat:
'T is found beneath the mercy-seat.

2 There is a place where Jesus sheds
  The oil of gladness on our heads,—
A place than all besides more sweet:
It is the blood-bought mercy-seat.

3 There is a scene where spirits blend,
  Where friend holds fellowship with
    friend;
Though sundered far, by faith they meet
Around one common mercy-seat.

4 There, there, on eagle wings we soar,
  And sense and sin molest no more,
And heaven comes down our souls to
    greet,
And glory crowns the mercy-seat.

5 Oh, let my hand forget her skill,
  My tongue be silent, cold and still,
This throbbing heart forget to beat,
If I forget the mercy-seat.

124 (368) C. M. C. WESLEY.

Before an Awakening Sermon.

COME, O thou all-victorious Lord,
  Thy power to us make known;
Strike with the hammer of thy word,
And break these hearts of stone.

2 O that we all might now begin
  Our foolishness to mourn!
And turn at once from every sin,
And to the Saviour turn.

3 Give us ourselves and thee to know
  In this our gracious day :
Repentance unto life bestow,
And take our sins away.

4 Convince us first of unbelief,
  And freely then release:
Fill every soul with sacred grief,
And then with sacred peace.

5 Our desp'rate state through sin declare,
  And speak our sins forgiven :
By perfect holiness prepare,
And take us up to heaven.

125 (369) L. M. C. WESLEY.

Before an Inviting Sermon.

SHEPHERD of souls, with pitying eye,
  The thousands of our Israel see ;
To thee, in their behalf, we cry,
  Ourselves but newly found in thee.

2 See where o'er desert wastes they err,
  And neither food nor feeder have ;
Nor fold nor place of refuge near ;
  For no man cares their souls to save.

3 Thy people, Lord, are sold for naught;
  Nor know they their Redeemer nigh :
They perish whom thyself hast bought;
  Their souls for lack of knowledge die.

4 Why should the foe thy purchase seize?
  Remember, Lord, thy dying groans :
The meed of all thy suff'rings these :
  O claim them for thy ransomed ones!

5 Still let the publicans draw near :
  Open the door of faith and heaven ;
And grant their hearts thy word to hear,
  And witness all their sins forgiven.

5 *

126 (370) C. M. C. WESLEY.

Before an Inviting Sermon.

JESUS, Redeemer of mankind,
  Display thy saving power ;
Thy mercy let these outcasts find,
  And know their gracious hour.

2 Ah! give them, Lord, a longer space,
  Nor suddenly consume ;
But let them take the proffered grace,
And flee the wrath to come.

3 O wouldst thou cast a pitying look,
  Ah! goodness as thou art,
Like that which faithless Peter's broke,
  On every stony heart !

4 Who thee beneath their feet have trod,
  And crucified afresh,
Touch with thine all-victorious blood,
And turn the stone to flesh.

5 Open their eyes thy cross to see,
  Their ears to hear thy cries :
Sinner, thy Saviour weeps for thee,
For thee he weeps and dies.

127 (371) C. M. C. WESLEY.

Before an Inviting Sermon.

JESUS, thou all-redeeming Lord,
  Thy blessing we implore ;
Open the door to preach thy word,
  The great effectual door.

2 Gather the outcasts in, and save
  From sin and Satan's power ;
And let them now acceptance have,
  And know their gracious hour.

3 Lover of souls ! thou know'st to prize
  What thou hast bought so dear :
Come, then, and in thy people's eyes,
  With all thy wounds appear !

4 Appear, as when of old confessed,
  The suff'ring Son of God ;
And let them see thee in thy vest,
  But newly dipped in blood.

5 The hardness from their hearts remove,
  Thou who for all hast died ;
Show them the tokens of thy love,
Thy feet, thy hands, thy side.

128 **(363)** C. M.   COWPER.

Before Preaching to the Young.

GRACE is a plant, where'er it grows,
Of pure and heavenly root:
But fairest in the youngest shows,
And yields the sweetest fruit.

2 Ye careless ones, O hear betimes
The voice of sovereign love!
Your youth is stained with many crimes,
But mercy reigns above.

3 True, you are young, but there's a stone
Within the youngest breast,
Or half the crimes which you have done
Would rob you of your rest.

4 For you the public prayer is made,
O join the public prayer!
For you the secret tear is shed,
O shed yourselves a tear!

5 We pray that you may early prove
The Spirit's power to teach;
You cannot be too young to love
That Jesus whom we preach.

129 **(365)** C. M.   GIBBONS.

Eccles. xii. 1.

IN the soft season of thy youth,
In nature's smiling bloom,
Ere age arrives, and trembling waits
Its summons to the tomb, —
Remember thy Creator now;
For him thy powers employ;
Make him thy fear, thy love, thy hope,
Thy confidence and joy.

2 He shall defend and guide thy youth
Through life's uncertain sea,
Till thou art landed on the coast
Of blessed eternity.
Then seek the Lord betimes, and choose
The path of heavenly truth:
This earth affords no lovelier sight
Than a religious youth.

130 **(364)** C. M.   DODDRIDGE.

Before Preaching to the Young.

YE hearts with youthful vigor warm,
In smiling crowds draw near,
And turn from every mortal charm,
A Saviour's voice to hear.

2 He, Lord of all the worlds on high,
Stoops to converse with you;
And lays his radiant glories by,
Your friendship to pursue.

3 "The soul that longs to see my face,
Is sure my love to gain;
And those that early seek my grace,
Shall never seek in vain."

4 What object, Lord, my soul should move,
If once compared with thee?
What beauty should command my love,
Like what in Christ I see?

5 Away, ye false, delusive toys,
Vain tempters of the mind!
'T is here I fix my lasting choice,
And here true bliss I find.

131 **(792)** C. M.   GILBERT.

For a Commencement.

WHILE we with fear and hope survey
This youthful, blooming throng,
And little know th' eventful way
Their steps may pass along, —

2 One day is as a thousand years,
Eternal God, to thee,
And present to thine eye appears
Their whole futurity.

3 Thou seest temptation's subtle thread,
Or torture's fiery test:
'Mid scenes of pleasure, or of dread,
Screen thou th' unguarded breast.

4 Saviour! through each portentous
change,
And dangers yet untrod,
Where'er they rest, where'er they range,
Be thou their present God!

132 (376) S. M.   C. WESLEY.

Praying for Repentance.

O THAT I could repent!
  O that I could believe!
Thou, by thy voice omnipotent,
  The rock in sunder cleave:
Thou, by thy two-edged sword,
  My soul and spirit part;
Strike with the hammer of thy word,
  And break my stubborn heart.

2 Saviour and Prince of peace,
  The double grace bestow:
Unloose the bands of wickedness,
  And let the captive go:
Grant me my sins to feel,
  And then the load remove:
Wound, and pour in, my wounds to heal,
  The balm of pard'ning love.

3 This is thy will, I know,
  That I should holy be;
Should let my sins this moment go,
  This moment turn to thee:
O might I now embrace
  Thy all-sufficient power!
And never more to sin give place,
  And never grieve thee more!

133 (377) C. M.   C. WESLEY.

Praying for Repentance.

O FOR that tenderness of heart
  Which bows before the Lord,
Acknowledging how just thou art,
  And trembling at thy word!
O for those humble, contrite tears,
  Which from repentance flow;
That consciousness of guilt which fears
  The long-suspended blow!

2 Saviour, to me in pity give
  The sensible distress;
The pledge thou wilt at last receive,
  And bid me die in peace:
Wilt from the dreadful day remove,
  Before the evil come:
My spirit hide with saints above,
  My body in the tomb.

134 (398) S. M.   C. WESLEY.

Struggling after Christ.

AH! whither should I go,
  Burdened, and sick, and faint!
To whom should I my troubles show,
  And pour out my complaint?
My Saviour bids me come;
  Ah! why do I delay?
He calls the weary sinner home,
  And yet from him I stay!

2 What is it keeps me back,
  From which I cannot part?
Which will not let the Saviour take
  Possession of my heart!
Some cursed thing unknown
  Must surely lurk within:
Some idol which I will not own,
  Some secret bosom-sin.

3 Jesus, the hindrance show,
  Which I have feared to see;
And let me now consent to know
  What keeps me back from thee.
Searcher of hearts, in mine
  Thy trying power display;
Into its darkest corners shine,
  And take the veil away.

135 (945) C. M.   W. M. BUNTING.

After Sermon on Sabbath Evening.

O BLESSED, blessed sounds of grace,
  Still echoing in my ear!
Glad is the hour, and loved the place,—
  'But whence my sudden fear?
What if a sternly righteous doom
  Have sealed this call my last?
Before me sickness,—death,—a tomb;
  Behind, th' unpardoned past.

2 My Sabbath suns may all have set,
  My Sabbath scenes be o'er;
The place, at least, where we are met,
  May know my steps no more.
The prophet of the cross may ne'er
  Again preach peace to me;
The voice of interceding prayer
  A farewell voice may be.

ZALMONAH. 7s, 6s, & 8s.

136 (379) 7s, 6s, & 8.

Praying for Repentance.

JESUS, let thy pitying eye
  Call back a wand'ring sheep;
False to thee, like Peter, I
  Would fain like Peter weep.
Let me be by grace restored;
  On me be all long-suff'ring shown;
Turn, and look upon me, Lord,
  And break my heart of stone.

2 Saviour, Prince, enthroned above,
  Repentance to impart,
Give me, through thy dying love,
  The humble, contrite heart:
Give, what I have long implored,
  A portion of thy grief unknown;
Turn, and look upon me, Lord,
  And break my heart of stone.

3 For thine own compassion's sake,
  The gracious wonder show;
Cast my sins behind thy back,
  And wash me white as snow:
If thy bowels now are stirred,
  If now I do myself bemoan,
Turn, and look upon me, Lord,
  And break my heart of stone.

137 (575) 7s, 6s, & 8. C. WESLEY.

Only Jesus.

VAIN, delusive world, adieu,
  With all of creature good!
Only Jesus I pursue,
  Who bought me with his blood!
All thy pleasures I forego,
  I trample on thy wealth and pride:
Only Jesus will I know,
  And Jesus crucified.

2 Other knowledge I disdain,
  'T is all but vanity:
Christ, the Lamb of God, was slain,
  He tasted death for me!
Me to save from endless woe
  The sin-atoning Victim died!
Only Jesus will I know,
  And Jesus crucified!

3 Here will I set up my rest;
  My fluctuating heart
From the haven of his breast
  Shall never more depart:
Whither should a sinner go?
  His wounds for me stand open wide:
Only Jesus will I know,
  And Jesus crucified!

138 **(381)** L. M.   WATTS.

Psalm li. 5-8.

LORD, we are vile, conceived in sin,
And born unholy and unclean:
Sprung from the man whose guilty fall
Corrupts his race, and taints us all.

2 Soon as we draw our infant breath,
The seeds of sin grow up for death:
Thy law demands a perfect heart,
But we're defiled in every part.

3 Great God, create my heart anew,
And form my spirit pure and true:
O make me wise betimes to see
My danger and my remedy!

4 Behold, I fall before thy face:
My only refuge is thy grace:
No outward forms can make me clean:
The leprosy lies deep within.

5 Jesus, my God, thy blood alone
Hath power sufficient to atone:
Thy blood can make me white as snow:
No Jewish types could cleanse me so.

6 While guilt disturbs and breaks my peace,
Nor flesh nor soul hath rest or ease:
Lord, let me hear thy pard'ning voice,
And make my broken heart rejoice.

139 **(383)** L. M.   WATTS.

Psalm li. 13-19.

A BROKEN heart, my God, my King,
To thee a sacrifice I bring:
The God of grace will ne'er despise
A broken heart for sacrifice.

2 My soul lies humbled in the dust,
And owns thy dreadful sentence just:
Look down, O Lord, with pitying eye,
And save the soul condemned to die.

3 Then will I teach the world thy ways,
Sinners shall learn thy sovereign grace;
I'll lead them to my Saviour's blood,
And they shall praise a pard'ning God.

4 O may thy love inspire my tongue!
Salvation shall be all my song;
And all my powers shall join to bless
The Lord, my strength and righteousness.

140 **(388)** C. M.   C. WESLEY.

Seeking the Power.

STILL, for thy loving-kindness, Lord,
I in thy temple wait:
I look to find thee in thy word,
Or at thy table meet.

2 Here in thine own appointed ways,
I wait to learn thy will;
Silent I stand before thy face,
And hear thee say, "Be still!

3 "Be still! and know that I am God!"
'T is all I live to know;
To feel the virtue of thy blood,
And spread its praise below!

4 I wait my vigor to renew,
Thine image to retrieve!
The veil of outward things pass through,
And gasp in thee to live.

141 **(394)** S. M.   C. WESLEY.

Surrendering the Heart.

WHEN shall thy love constrain,
And force me to thy breast?
When shall my soul return again
To her eternal rest?

2 Ah! what avails my strife,
My wand'ring to and fro?
Thou hast the words of endless life:
Ah! whither should I go?

3 Thy condescending grace
To me did freely move:
It calls me still to seek thy face,
And stoops to ask my love.

4 Lord, at thy feet I fall,
I groan to be set free:
I fain would now obey the call,
And give up all for thee.

5 To rescue me from woe,
Thou didst with all things part,
Didst lead a suff'ring life below,
To gain my worthless heart.

6 My worthless heart to gain,
The God of all that breathe
Was found in fashion as a man,
And died a cursed death.

142 (382) L. M.   WATTS.

Psalm li. 9-12.

O THOU, who hear'st when sinners
      cry,
Though all my crimes before thee lie,
Behold them not with angry look,
But blot their mem'ry from thy book.

2 Create my nature pure within,
And form my soul averse from sin :
Let thy good Spirit ne'er depart,
Nor hide thy presence from my heart.

3 I cannot live without thy light,
Cast out and banished from thy sight
Thy holy joys, my God, restore,
And guard me that I fall no more.

4 Though I have grieved thy Spirit, Lord,
Thy help and comfort still afford ;
And let a wretch come near thy throne,
To plead the merits of thy Son.

143 (380) L. M.   WATTS.

Psalm li. 1-4.

SHOW pity, Lord, O Lord, forgive,
      Let a repenting rebel live :
Are not thy mercies large and free?
May not a sinner trust in thee?

2 My crimes are great, but don't surpass
The power and glory of thy grace :
Great God, thy nature hath no bound,
So let thy pard'ning love be found.

3 O wash my soul from every sin !
And make my guilty conscience clean !
Here on my heart the burden lies,
And past offences pain mine eyes.

4 My lips with shame my sins confess,
Against thy law, against thy grace :
Lord, should thy judgments grow severe
I am condemned, but thou art clear.

5 Should sudden vengeance seize my
      breath,
I must pronounce thee just in death ;
And if my soul were sent to hell,
Thy righteous law approves it well.

6 Yet save a trembling sinner, Lord,
Whose hope, still hov'ring round thy
      word,
Would light on some sweet promise
      there,
Some sure support against despair.

144 (391) C. M.   ADDISON.

Contrition.

WHEN, rising from the bed of death,
      O'erwhelmed with guilt and fear,
I view my Maker face to face,
      O how shall I appear !

2 If yet, while pardon may be found,
      And mercy may be sought,
My soul with inward horror shrinks,
      And trembles at the thought:

3 When thou, O Lord, shalt stand disclosed
      In majesty severe,
And sit in judgment on my soul,
      O how shall I appear !

4 O may my broken, contrite heart,
      Timely my sins lament,
And early with repentant tears
      Eternal woe prevent.

145 (393) L. M.   HART.

Hardness of Heart Lamented.

O FOR a glance of heavenly day,
      To take this stubborn heart away,
And thaw with beams of love divine,
This heart, this frozen heart of mine !

2 The rocks can rend ; the earth can quake ;
The seas can roar ; the mountains shake :
Of feeling, all things show some sign,
But this unfeeling heart of mine.

3 To hear the sorrows thou hast felt,
O Lord, an adamant would melt !
But I can read each moving line,
And nothing moves this heart of mine.

4 Thy judgments, too, unmoved I hear,
(Amazing thought !) which devils fear:
Goodness and wrath in vain combine
To stir this stupid heart of mine.

5 But something yet can do the deed ;
And that blessed something much I need :
Thy Spirit can from dross refine,
And melt and change this heart of mine.

146 **(395)** S. M.

Surrendering the Heart.

AND can I yet delay
  My little all to give?
To tear my soul from earth away
For Jesus to receive?

2 Nay, but I yield, I yield!
  I can hold out no more:
I sink, by dying love compelled,
And own thee conqueror!

3 Though late, I all forsake;
  My friends, my all resign:
Gracious Redeemer, take, O take,
And seal me ever thine!

4 Come, and possess me whole,
  Nor hence again remove:
Settle and fix my wav'ring soul
With all thy weight of love.

5 My one desire be this,
  Thy only love to know;
To seek and taste no other bliss,
No other good below.

6 My life, my portion thou,
  Thou all-sufficient art:
My hope, my heavenly treasure, now
Enter and keep my heart.

147 **(431)** S. M. C. WESLEY.

The Plea.

JESUS, my Lord, attend
  Thy feeble creature's cry;
And show thyself the sinner's Friend,
And set me up on high.

2 From hell's oppressive power
  My struggling soul release,
And to thy Father's grace restore,
And to thy perfect peace.

3 Rivers of life divine
  From thee, their fountain, flow;
And all who know that love of thine,
The joy of angels know.

4 That thou canst here forgive,
  Grant me to testify;
And justified by faith to live,
And in that faith to die.

148 **(436)** 8s & 6s. C. WESLEY.

Panting for the Love of God.

O LOVE Divine, how sweet thou art!
  When shall I find my willing heart
  All taken up by thee?
I thirst, I faint, I die to prove
The greatness of redeeming love,
  The love of Christ to me.

2 Stronger his love than death or hell;
Its riches are unsearchable:
  The first-born sons of light
Desire in vain its depths to see;
They cannot reach the mystery,
  The length, the breadth, and height.

3 God only knows the love of God:
O that it now were shed abroad
  In this poor stony heart!
For love I sigh, for love I pine:
This only portion, Lord, be mine!
  Be mine this better part!

4 O that I could for ever sit
With Mary at the Master's feet!
  Be this my happy choice:
My only care, delight, and bliss,
My joy, my heaven on earth, be this,
  To hear the Bridegroom's voice!

5 O that with humbled Peter, I
Could weep, believe, and thrice reply,
  My faithfulness to prove,
Thou know'st, for all to thee is known,
Thou know'st, O Lord, and thou alone,
  Thou know'st that thee I love.

6 O that I could with favored John
Recline my weary head upon
  The dear Redeemer's breast!
From care, and sin, and sorrow free,
Give me, O Lord, to find in thee
  My everlasting rest!

7 Thy only love do I require,
Nothing in earth beneath desire,
  Nothing in heaven above:
Let earth, and heaven, and all things go,
Give me thy only love to know,
  Give me thy only love.

GAVIN. S. M.

149 (595) S. M.　　C. WESLEY.

Keeping the Charge of the Lord.

A CHARGE to keep I have,
　A God to glorify;
A never-dying soul to save,
　And fit it for the sky;

2 To serve the present age,
　My calling to fulfil; —
O may it all my powers engage
　To do my Master's will!

3 Arm me with jealous care,
　As in thy sight to live;
And O thy servant, Lord, prepare,
　A strict account to give!

4 Help me to watch and pray,
　And on thyself rely,
Assured, if I my trust betray,
　· I shall for ever die.

Doxology.

Give to the Father praise;
Give glory to the Son;
And to the Spirit of his grace
Be equal honor done.

150 (378) S. M.　　C. WESLEY.

Praying for Repentance.

O THAT I could revere
　My much-offended God!
O that I could but stand in fear
　Of thy afflicting rod!

2 If mercy cannot draw,
　Thou by thy threat'ning move:
And keep an abject soul in awe,
　That will not yield to love.

3 Let me with horror fly
　From every sinful snare;
Nor ever in my Judge's eye
　My Judge's anger dare.

4 Thou great, tremendous God,
　The conscious awe impart;
The grace be now on me bestowed,
　The tender fleshly heart:

5 For Jesus' sake alone,
　The stony heart remove:
And melt, at last, O melt me down,
　Into the mould of love!

151 (396) L. M.   C. WESLEY.
Feeling after Christ.

WHEN, gracious Lord, when shall it
   be
That I shall find my all in thee?
The fulness of thy promise prove,
The seal of thine eternal love?

2 A poor blind child I wander here,
If haply I may feel thee near:
O dark! dark! dark! I still must say,
Amidst the blaze of gospel day.

3 Thee, only thee, I fain would find,
And cast the world and flesh behind:
Thou, only thou, to me be given,
Of all thou hast in earth or heaven.

4 When from the arm of flesh set free,
Jesus, my soul shall fly to thee:
Jesus, when I have lost my all,
I shall upon thy bosom fall.

152 (397) L. M.   C. WESLEY.
Concluded.

WHOM man forsakes thou wilt not
   leave,
Ready the outcasts to receive;
Though all my simpleness I own,
And all my faults to thee are known.

2 Ah! wherefore did I ever doubt?
Thou wilt in no wise cast me out,—
A helpless soul that comes to thee,
With only sin and misery.

3 Lord, I am sick,— my sickness cure:
I want,— do thou enrich the poor:
Under thy mighty hand I stoop,
O lift the abject sinner up!

153 (387) C. M.
Having the Form of Godliness.

LONG have I seem'd to serve thee, Lord,
   With unavailing pain:
Fasted, and pray'd, and read thy word,
And heard it preach'd in vain.

2 Oft did I with th' assembly join,
   And near thy altar drew;
A form of godliness was mine,
The power I never knew.

3 I rested in the outward law,
Nor knew its deep design:
The length and breadth I never saw,
And height, of love divine.

4 To please thee thus at length I see,
Vainly I hoped and strove:
For what are outward things to thee,
Unless they spring from love?

5 I see the perfect law requires
Truth in the inward parts;
Our full consent, our whole desires,
Our undivided hearts.

6 But I of means have made my boast,
Of means an idol made:
The spirit in the letter lost,
The substance in the shade.

7 Where am I now?—what is my hope?
What can my weakness do?
Jesus, to thee my soul looks up:
'T is thou must make it new.

154 (403) C. M.   C. WESLEY.
The Earnest Suit.

O THAT I could my Lord receive,
   Who did the world redeem;
Who gave his life that I might live
A life concealed in him!

2 O that I could the blessing prove,
My heart's extreme desire!
Live happy in my Saviour's love,
And in his arms expire!

3 In number to ten thousand prayers,
Thou pard'ning God, descend:
Number me with salvation's heirs,
My sins and troubles end.

4 Nothing I ask or want beside,
Of all in earth or heaven,
But let me feel thy blood applied,
And live and die forgiven.

155 (404) 7s.   C. WESLEY.
Why not Now?

WHY not now, my God, my God?
   Ready if thou always art,
Make in me thy mean abode,
Take possession of my heart:
If thou canst so greatly bow,
Friend of sinners, why not now?

2 God of love, in this thy day,
For thyself to thee I cry;
Dying,— if thou still delay,
Must I not for ever die?
Enter now thy poorest home;
Now, my utmost Saviour, come!

156 (406) C. M.   C. WESLEY.
The Prisoner of Hope.

THOU hidden God, for whom I groan—
Till thou thyself declare,
God, inaccessible, unknown,—
Regard a sinner's prayer!
A sinner welt'ring in his blood,
Unpurged and unforgiven;
Far distant from the living God,
As far as hell from heaven.

2 An unregen'rate child of man,
To thee for faith I call;
Pity thy fallen creature's pain,
And raise me from my fall.
The darkness which through thee I feel,
Thou only canst remove;
Thy own eternal power reveal,
Thy everlasting love.

157 (407) C. M.   C. WESLEY.
The Prisoner of Hope.

LET the redeemed give thanks and
praise,
To a forgiving God!
My feeble voice I cannot raise,
'Till washed in Jesus' blood:

2 Till, at thy coming from above,
My mountain-sins depart,
And fear gives place to filial love,
And peace o'erflows my heart.

3 Pris'ner of hope, I still attend
Th' appearance of my Lord,
These endless doubts and fears to end,
And speak my soul restored:

4 Restored by reconciling grace;
With present pardon blessed;
And fitted by true holiness
For my eternal rest.

5 Now, Lord, if thou art power, descend,
The mountain, sin, remove;
My unbelief and troubles end,
If thou art truth and love.

6 Speak, Jesus, speak into my heart,
What thou for me hast done!
A ray of living faith impart,
And God is all my own.

158 (675) S. M.   C. WESLEY.
The End of Life.

O THOU that wouldst not have
One wretched sinner die;
Who diedst thyself, my soul to save
From endless misery!
Show me the way to shun
Thy dreadful wrath severe;
That when thou comest on thy throne,
I may with joy appear!

2 Thou art thyself the way,
Thyself in me reveal;
So shall I spend my life's short day
Obedient to thy will:
So shall I love my God,
Because he first loved me;
And praise thee in thy bright abode
To all eternity.

159 (683) C. M.   WATTS.
The Sinner's End.

MY thoughts on awful subjects roll,—
Damnation and the dead;
What horrors seize the guilty soul
Upon a dying bed!

2 Ling'ring about these mortal shores,
She makes a long delay;
Till, like a flood with rapid force,
Death sweeps the wretch away.

3 Then, swift and dreadful, she descends
Down to the fiery coast,
Among abominable fiends,
Herself a frighted ghost.

4 There endless crowds of sinners lie,
And darkness makes their chains;
Tortured with keen despair, they cry;
Yet wait for fiercer pains.

5 Not all their anguish and their blood
For their old guilt atones;
Nor the compassion of a God
Shall hearken to their groans.

160 (411) L. M. C. WESLEY.

Self-despair.

LORD, I despair myself to heal:
　I see my sin, but cannot feel,—
I cannot, till thy Spirit blow,
And bid th' obedient waters flow.

2 'T is thine a heart of flesh to give:
Thy gifts I only can receive;
Here, then, to thee I all resign,
To draw, redeem, and seal — are thine.

3 With simple faith on thee I call;
My light, my life, my Lord, my all:
I wait the moving of the pool;
I wait the word that speaks me whole.

4 Speak, gracious Lord, my sickness cure;
Make my infected nature pure:
Peace, righteousness, and joy, impart,
And pour thyself into my heart!

161 (412) L. M. C. WESLEY.

Fleeing to the Sinner's Friend.

JESUS, the sinner's Friend, to thee,
　Lost and undone, for aid I flee:
Weary of earth, myself, and sin;
Open thine arms and take me in.

2 Pity and heal my sin-sick soul;
'T is thou alone canst make me whole:
Fall'n, till in me thine image shine,
And lost I am till thou art mine.

3 Awake, the woman's conqu'ring Seed,
Awake, and bruise the serpent's head!
Tread down thy foes, with power control
The beast and devil in my soul.

4 What shall I say thy grace to move?
Lord, I am sin,—but thou art love:
I give up every plea beside,
"Lord, I am lost — but thou hast died."

162 (413) L. M. C. WESLEY.

The Good Physician.

JESUS, thy far-extended fame
　My drooping soul exults to hear;
Thy name, thy all-restoring name,
Is music in a sinner's ear.

2 Sinners of old thou didst receive,
With comfortable words, and kind,
Their sorrows cheer, their wants relieve,
Heal the diseased, and cure the blind.

3 And art thou not the Saviour still,
In every place and age the same?
Hast thou forgot thy gracious skill, .
Or lost the virtue of thy name?

4 Faith in thy changeless name I have,
The good, the kind Physician, thou
Art able now our souls to save,
Art willing to restore them now.

163 (414) L. M. C. WESLEY.

"Heal my soul."

O THOU, whom once they flocked to
　hear!
Thy words to hear, thy power to feel;
Suffer the sinners to draw near,
And graciously receive us still.

2 They that be whole, thyself hast said,
No need of a physician have;
But I am sick, and want thine aid,
And ask thine utmost power to save.

3 Thy power, and truth, and love divine,
The same from age to age endure:
A word, a gracious word of thine,
The most invet'rate plague can cure.

4 Helpless, howe'er, my spirit lies,
And long hath languished at the pool:
A word of thine shall make it rise,
Shall speak me in a moment whole.

164 (415) C. M. C. WESLEY.

Miracles of Grace.

JESUS, if still thou art to-day,
　As yesterday, the same,
Present to heal, in me display
The virtue of thy name!

2 If still thou go'st about to do
Thy needy creatures good,
On me, that I thy praise may show,
Be all thy wonders showed.

165 (417) C. M.   C. WESLEY.
Urgent Pleadings.

O THAT thou wouldst the heavens
    rend,
In majesty come down;
Thine arm omnipotent extend,
And seize me for thine own!

2 Descend, and let thy lightnings burn
The stubble of thy foe:
My sins o'erturn, o'erturn, o'erturn,
And make the mountains flow!

3 Thou my impetuous spirit guide,
And curb my headstrong will:
Thou only canst drive back the tide,
And bid the sun stand still.

4 What though I cannot break my chain,
Or e'er throw off my load?
The things impossible to men
Are possible to God.

166 (418) C. M.   C. WESLEY.
Concluded.

JESUS! Redeemer, Saviour, Lord,
The weary sinner's Friend;
Come to my help, pronounce the word,
And bid my troubles end.

2. Deliv'rance to my soul proclaim,
And life and liberty:
Shed forth the virtue of thy name,
And Jesus prove to me!

3 Faith to be healed thou know'st I have,
For thou that faith hast given:
Thou canst, thou wilt, the sinner save,
And make me meet for heaven.

4 Thou canst o'ercome this heart of mine;
Thou wilt victorious prove;
For everlasting strength is thine,
And everlasting love.

167 (420) C. M.   C. WESLEY.
Praying for Faith.

WITH glorious clouds encompassed
    round,
Whom angels dimly see,
Will the Unsearchable be found,
Or God appear to me?

2 Will he forsake his throne above,
Himself to worms impart?
Answer, thou Man of grief and love!
And speak it to my heart.

3 In manifested love explain
Thy wonderful design:
What meant the suff'ring Son of man,
The streaming blood divine?

4 Before my eyes of faith confessed,
Stand forth a slaughtered Lamb;
And wrap me in thy crimson vest,
And tell me all thy name.

168 (435) C. M.   NEWTON.
Subdued by the Cross.

IN evil long I took delight,
    Unawed by shame or fear;
Till a new object struck my sight,
And stopped my wild career.

2 I saw one hanging on a tree,
In agonies and blood,
Who fixed his languid eyes on me,
As near his cross I stood.

3 Sure, never to my latest breath
Can I forget that look:
It seemed to charge me with his death,
Though not a word he spoke.

4 My conscience felt, and owned the guilt,
And plunged me in despair:
I saw my sins his blood had spilt,
And helped to nail him there.

5 A second look he gave, which said,
"I freely all forgive;
This blood is for thy ransom paid;
I die that thou may'st live."

169 (425) C. M.   WATTS.
Surrendering at the Cross.

ALAS! and did my Saviour bleed?
  And did my Sovereign die?
Would he devote that sacred head
  For such a worm as I?

2 Was it for crimes that I have done
  He groaned upon the tree?
Amazing pity! grace unknown!
  And love beyond degree!

3 Well might the sun in darkness hide,
  And shut his glories in,
When Christ, the mighty Maker, died
  For man, the creature's sin!

4 Thus might I hide my blushing face,
  While his dear cross appears;
Dissolve my heart in thankfulness,
  And melt mine eyes to tears.

5 But drops of grief can ne'er repay
  The debt of love I owe:
Here, Lord, I give myself away,
  'T is all that I can do.

170 (427) C. M.   . NEWTON.
The Effort.

APPROACH, my soul, the mercy-seat,
  Where Jesus answers prayer;
There humbly fall before his feet,
  For none can perish there.

2 Thy promise is my only plea,
  With this I venture nigh:
Thou call'st the burdened soul to thee,
  And such, O Lord, am I.

3 Bowed down beneath a load of sin,
  By Satan sorely pressed,
By wars without, and fears within,
  I come to thee for rest.

4 Be thou my shield and hiding-place,
  That, sheltered near thy side,
I may my fierce accuser face,
  And tell him thou hast died.

5 O, wondrous love, to bleed and die,
  To bear the cross and shame,
That guilty sinners, such as I,
  Might plead his precious name!

6 *

171 (428) L. M.   CENNICK.
"I am the way."

JESUS, my all, to heaven is gone,
  He whom I fix my hopes upon;
His track I see, and I 'll pursue
  The narrow way, till him I view.

2 The way the holy prophets went,
  The road that leads from banishment,
The King's highway of holiness,
  I 'll go, for all his paths are peace.

3 This is the way I long have sought,
  And mourned because I found it not:
My grief a burden long has been,
  Because I was not saved from sin.

4 The more I strove against its power,
  I felt its weight and guilt the more;
Till late I heard my Saviour say,
  "Come hither, soul, I AM THE WAY."

5 Lo! glad I come, and thou, blessed Lamb,
  Shalt take me to thee as I am;
Nothing but sin have I to give,
  Nothing but love shall I receive.

6 Then will I tell to sinners round
  What a dear Saviour I have found;
I 'll point to thy redeeming blood,
  And say, "Behold the way to God!"

172 (424) C. M.   C. WESLEY.
Praying for Faith.

FATHER, I stretch my hands to thee,
  No other help I know;
If thou withdraw thyself from me,
  Ah! whither shall I go?

2 What did thine only Son endure,
  Before I drew my breath!
What pain, what labor to secure
  My soul from endless death!

3 O Jesus, could I this believe,
  I now should feel thy power!
Now my poor soul thou wouldst retrieve,
  Nor let me wait one hour.

4 Author of faith, to thee I lift
  My weary, longing eyes;
O let me now receive that gift,
  My soul without it dies!

E

173 (433) 7s.   C. WESLEY.
Refuge in Christ.

JESUS, lover of my soul,
    Let me to thy bosom fly,
While the nearer waters roll,
While the tempest still is high:
Hide me, O my Saviour, hide,
    Till the storm of life be past;
Safe into the haven guide,
    O receive my soul at last!

2 Other refuge have I none,
    Hangs my helpless soul on thee:
Leave, ah! leave me not alone,
    Still support and comfort me!
All my trust on thee is stayed,
All my help from thee I bring,
Cover my defenceless head
    With the shadow of thy wing.

3 Thou, O Christ, art all I want;
    More than all in thee I find:
Raise the fallen, cheer the faint,
    Heal the sick, and lead the blind.
Just and holy is thy name;
I am all unrighteousness:
False, and full of sin, I am;
    Thou art full of truth and grace.

4 Plenteous grace with thee is found,
    Grace to cover all my sin:
Let the healing streams abound,
    Make and keep me pure within:
Thou of life the fountain art;
    Freely let me take of thee:
Spring thou up within my heart,
    Rise to all eternity!

174 (939) 7s.   C. WESLEY.
For Reviving Grace.

LIGHT of life, seraphic fire,
    Love divine, thyself impart;
Every fainting soul inspire;
    Shine in every drooping heart:
Every mournful sinner cheer;
    Scatter all our guilty gloom:
Son of God, appear! appear!
    To thy human temples come.

2 Come in this accepted hour:
    Bring thy heavenly kingdom in:
Fill us with thy glorious power,
    Rooting out the seeds of sin:
Nothing more can we require,
We will covet nothing less:
Be thou all our hearts' desire,
    All our joy, and all our peace.

175 (676) S. M.   MONTGOMERY.
The Issues of Life and Death.

O WHERE shall rest be found,
    Rest for the weary soul?
'T were vain the ocean depths to sound,
    Or pierce to either pole:
The world can never give
    The bliss for which we sigh:
'T is not the whole of life to live,
    Nor all of death to die.

2 Beyond this vale of tears
    There is a life above,
Unmeasured by the flight of years;
    And all that life is love:—
There is a death whose pang
    Outlasts the fleeting breath;
O! what eternal horrors hang
    Around " the second death! "

3 Lord God of truth and grace,
    Teach us that death to shun,
Lest we be banished from thy face,
    And evermore undone.
Here would we end our quest:
    Alone are found in thee,
The life of perfect love, the rest
    Of immortality.

176 (545) 7s.   C. WESLEY.
Humble Aspiration.

WHEN, my Saviour, shall I be
    Perfectly resigned to thee?
Poor and vile in my own eyes,
Only in thy wisdom wise?

2 Only thee content to know,
Ignorant of all below?
Only guided by thy light;
Only mighty in thy might?

LUTHER'S. L. M. 6 lines. (Six 8s.) M. LUTHER.

177 (441) 8s.   C. WESLEY.

Wrestling Jacob.

COME, O thou Traveller unknown,
  Whom still I hold, but cannot see;
My company before is gone,
  And I am left alone with thee;
With thee all night I mean to stay,
And wrestle till the break of day.

2 I need not tell thee who I am;
  My sin and misery declare;
Thyself hast called me by my name,
  Look on thy hands and read it there;
But who, I ask thee, who art thou?
Tell me thy name, and tell me now.

3 In vain thou strugglest to get free,
  I never will unloose my hold:
Art thou the man that died for me?
  The secret of thy love unfold:
Wrestling, I will not let thee go,
Till I thy name, thy nature know.

4 Wilt thou not yet to me reveal
  Thy new, unutterable name?
Tell me, I still beseech thee, tell;
  To know it now resolved I am:
Wrestling, I will not let thee go,
Till I thy name, thy nature know.

5 What though my shrinking flesh com-
    plain,
  And murmur to contend so long?

I rise superior to my pain:
  When I am weak, then I am strong!
And when my all of strength shall fail,
I shall with the God-man prevail!

178 (929) 8s.   C. WESLEY.

The Universal Good Invoked.

COME, O thou universal Good!
  Balm of the wounded conscience,
    come!
The hungry, dying spirit's food,
  The weary, wand'ring pilgrim's home,
Haven to take the shipwrecked in,
My everlasting rest from sin!

2 Come, O my comfort and delight!
  My strength and health, my shield
    and sun;
My boast, and confidence, and might,
  My joy, my glory, and my crown;
My gospel hope, my calling's prize,
My tree of life, my paradise.

3 The secret of the Lord thou art,
  The mystery so long unknown,
Christ in a pure and perfect heart!
  The name inscribed in the white stone!
The life divine, the little leaven,
My precious pearl, my present heaven.

ORTONVILLE. C. M.

179 (449) C. M.　　Cowper.

The Backslider's Prayer.

O FOR a closer walk with God,
　A calm and heavenly frame;
A light to shine upon the road
　That leads me to the Lamb.

2 Where is the blessedness I knew
　When first I saw the Lord?
Where is the soul-refreshing view
　Of Jesus and his word?

3 What peaceful hours I once enjoyed!
　How sweet their mem'ry still!
But they have left an aching void
　The world can never fill.

4 Return, O holy Dove, return,
　Sweet messenger of rest!
I hate the sins that made thee mourn,
　And drove thee from my breast.

5 The dearest idol I have known,
　Whate'er that idol be,
Help me to tear it from thy throne,
　And worship only thee.

6 So shall my walk be close with God,
　Calm and serene my frame;
So purer light shall mark the road
　That leads me to the Lamb.

180 (421) C. M.　　Watts.

"Help thou my unbelief."

H OW sad our state by nature is!
　Our sin how deep it stains!
And Satan binds our captive souls
　Fast in his slavish chains.

2 But there's a voice of sovereign grace
　Sounds from the sacred word:
・Ho! ye despairing sinners, come,
　And trust a faithful Lord.

3 My soul obeys the gracious call,
　And runs to this relief:
I would believe thy promise, Lord,
　O help my unbelief!

4 To the blest fountain of thy blood,
　Incarnate God, I fly:
Here let me wash my spotted soul
　From crimes of deepest dye.

5 A guilty, weak, and helpless worm,
　Into thy arms I fall:
Be thou my strength and righteousness,
　My Jesus and my all.

Doxology.

Now let the Father, and the Son,
　And Spirit be adored,　　　[known,
Where there are works to make him
　Or saints to love the Lord.

PENTONVILLE. S. M.

Moderato.

181 (452) S. M.   C. WESLEY.

The Backslider's Complaint.

AND wilt thou yet be found?
  And may I still draw near?
Then listen to the plaintive sound
Of a poor sinner's prayer.

2 Jesus, thine aid afford,
    If still the same thou art:
  To thee I look, to thee, my Lord!
    Lift up a helpless heart.

3 Thou seest my troubled breast,
    The strugglings of my will,
  The foes that interrupt my rest,
    The agonies I feel.

4 The daily death I prove,
    Saviour, to thee is known:
  'T is worse than death my God to love,
    And not my God alone.

5 O my offended Lord,
    Restore my inward peace:
  I know thou canst pronounce the word,
    And bid the tempest cease!

182 (447) S. M.   C. WESLEY.

The Backslider's Return.

O JESUS! full of grace,
  To thee I make my moan:
Let me again behold thy face,
  Call home thy banished one.

2 Again my pardon seal,
    Again my soul restore,
  And freely my backslidings heal,
    And bid me sin no more.

3 Wilt thou not bid me rise?
    Speak, and my soul shall live:
  Forgive, my gasping spirit cries,
    Abundantly forgive.

4 For thine own mercy's sake,
    Relieve my wretchedness;
  And O, my pardon give me back,
    And give me back my peace!

5 Again thy love reveal,
    Restore that inward heaven:
  O grant me once again to feel,
    Through faith, my sins forgiven!

BENEVENTO. 7s.

183 (453) 7s.   C. WESLEY.
The Backslider's Plea.

DEPTH of mercy! can there be
Mercy still reserved for me?
Can my God his wrath forbear?
Me, the chief of sinners, spare?

2 I have long withstood his grace,
Long provoked him to his face;
Would not hearken to his calls;
Grieved him by a thousand falls.

3 Lo! I cumber still the ground:
Lo! an Advocate is found!
"Hasten not to cut him down:
Let this barren soul alone!"

4 Jesus speaks, and pleads his blood;
He disarms the wrath of God!
Now my Father's bowels move;
Justice lingers into love.

5 Kindled his relentings are;
Me he now delights to spare;
Cries, "How shall I give thee up?"
Lets the lifted thunder drop.

6 There for me the Saviour stands;
Shows his wounds, and spreads his hands:
God is love! I know, I feel;
Jesus weeps and loves me still.

184 (598) 7s.
Stability Sought.

JESUS, shall I never be
Firmly grounded upon thee?
Never by thy work abide?
Never in thy wounds reside?

2 O how wav'ring is my mind!
Tossed about with every wind!
O how quickly doth my heart
From the living God depart!

3 Jesus, let my nature feel
Thou art God unchangeable:
JAH, JEHOVAH, great I AM,
Speak unto my soul thy name.

4 Grant that every moment I
May believe and feel thee nigh,
Steadfastly behold thy face,
Stablished with abiding grace.

WELLS. L. M.

185 (526) L. M.   J. WESLEY.

Consecration.

COME, Saviour, Jesus, from above!
  Assist me with thy heavenly grace;
Empty my heart of earthly love,
  And for thyself prepare the place.

2 O let thy sacred presence fill,
  And set my longing spirit free,
Which pants to have no other will,
  But day and night to feast on thee.

3 While in this region here below,
  No other good will I pursue:
I'll bid this world of noise and show,
  With all its glitt'ring snares, adieu!

4 That path with humble speed I'll seek,
  In which my Saviour's footsteps shine,
Nor will I hear nor will I speak
  Of any other love but thine.

5 Henceforth may no profane delight
  Divide this consecrated soul;
Possess it, thou, who hast the right,
  As Lord and Master of the whole.

186 (518) L. M.   C. WESLEY.

Ezekiel xxxvi. 23–25.

GOD of all power, and truth, and grace,
  Which shall from age to age endure;
Whose word, when heaven and earth
    shall pass,
  Remains, and stands for ever sure:

2 Calmly to thee my soul looks up,
  And waits thy promises to prove,
The object of my steadfast hope,
  The seal of thy eternal love.

3 That I thy mercy may proclaim,
  That all mankind thy truth may see,
Hallow thy great and glorious name,
  And perfect holiness in me.

4 Thy sanctifying Spirit pour,
  To quench my thirst, and make me
    clean:
Now, Father, let the gracious shower
  Descend, and make me pure from
    sin.

GANGES. C. P. M.

187 (673) 8s & 6.   C. WESLEY.

The End of Life.

AND am I only born to die?
  And must I suddenly comply
With nature's stern decree?
What after death for me remains?
Celestial joys, or hellish pains,
  To all eternity!

2 How then ought I on earth to live,
While God prolongs the kind reprieve,
  And props the house of clay:
My sole concern, my single care,
To watch, and tremble, and prepare
  Against that fatal day!

3 No room for mirth or trifling here,
For worldly hope or worldly fear,
  If life so soon is gone;
If now the Judge is at the door,
And all mankind must stand before
  Th' inexorable throne!

4 No matter which my thoughts employ,
A moment's misery or joy;
  But O! when both shall end,
Where shall I find my destined place?
Shall I my everlasting days
  With fiends or angels spend?

5 Nothing is worth a thought beneath,
But how I may escape the death
  That never, never dies!
How make mine own election sure,
And when I fail on earth, secure
  A mansion in the skies.

6 Jesus, vouchsafe a pitying ray,
Be thou my guide, be thou my way,
  To glorious happiness!
Ah! write the pardon on my heart!
And whensoe'er I hence depart,
  Let me depart in peace!

188 (384)C. M.　　C. WESLEY.

The Resolve.

SHALL I, amidst a ghastly band,
　Dragged to the judgment seat,
Far on the left with horror stand,
My fearful doom to meet? —

2 Dissolved are nature's closest ties,
　And bosom-friends forgot,
When God, the just avenger cries,
Depart, I know you not! —

3 But must I from his glorious face,
　From all his saints retire?
But must I go to my own place
In everlasting fire? —

4 Ah! no; — I still may turn and live,
　For still his wrath delays;
He now vouchsafes a kind reprieve,
And offers me his grace.

5 I will accept his offers now :
　From every sin depart;
Perform my oft-repeated vow,
And render him my heart.

189 (689) C. M.　　C. WESLEY.

The Day of Judgment.

AND must I be to judgment brought,
　And answer in that day,
For every vain and idle thought
And every word I say?

2 Yes, every secret of my heart
　Shall shortly be made known,
And I receive my just desert
For all that I have done.

3 How careful, then, ought I to live!
　With what religious fear!
Who such a strict account must give
For my behavior here!

4 Thou awful Judge of quick and dead,
　The watchful power bestow;
So shall I to my ways take heed,
To all I speak or do.

5 If now thou standest at the door,
　O, let me feel thee near!
And make my peace with God, before
I at thy bar appear.

7

190 (402)L. M.　　C. WESLEY.

Awful Distress.

THOU Man of griefs, remember me,
　Who never canst thyself forget,
Thy last mysterious agony,
Thy fainting pangs and bloody sweat!

2 When wrestling in the strength of prayer,
　Thy spirit sunk beneath its load,
Thy feeble flesh abhorred to bear
The wrath of an almighty God.

3 Father, if I may call thee so,
　Regard my fearful heart's desire;
Remove this load of guilty woe,
Nor let me in my sins expire!

4 To thee my last distress I bring;
　The heightened fear of death I find;
The tyrant, brandishing his sting,
Appears, and hell is close behind.

5 I deprecate that death alone,
　That endless banishment from thee:
O save, and give me to thy Son,
Who trembled, wept, and bled for me!

191 (719) C. M.　　WATTS.

Eternal Death.

THAT awful day will surely come,
　Th' appointed hour makes haste,
When I must stand before my Judge,
And pass the solemn test.

2 Jesus, thou Source of all my joys,
　Thou Ruler of my heart,
How could I bear to hear thy voice
Pronounce the sound, " Depart!"

3 The thunder of that awful word
　Would so torment my ear,
'T would tear my soul asunder, Lord,
With most tormenting fear.

4 What, to be banished from my Lord,
　And yet forbid to die!
To linger in eternal pain,
And death for ever fly!

5 O wretched state of deep despair,
　To see my God remove,
And fix my doleful station where
I must not taste his love!

HAMBURG. L. M.

192 (697) L. M.　　　WATTS.

Heaven. Psalm xvii. 15.

WHAT sinners value, I resign;
Lord, 'tis enough that thou art
mine:
I shall behold thy blissful face,
And stand complete in righteousness.

2 This life's a dream, an empty show;
But the bright world to which I go
Hath joys substantial and sincere:
When shall I wake and find me there?

3 O, glorious hour! O, blest abode!
I shall be near, and like, my God;
And flesh and sin no more control
The sacred pleasures of the soul.

4 My flesh shall slumber in the ground
Till the last trumpet's joyful sound;
Then burst the chains with sweet sur-
prise,
And in my Saviour's image rise.

193 (687) L. M.　　　DODDRIDGE.

Desiring to Depart.

WHILE on the verge of life I stand,
And view the scene on either
hand,
My spirit struggles with my clay,
And longs to wing its flight away.

2 Where Jesus dwells my soul would
be;
It faints my much-loved Lord to see:
Earth, twine no more about my heart,
For 'tis far better to depart.

3 Come, ye angelic envoys, come,
And lead the willing pilgrim home:
Ye know the way to Jesus' throne,
Source of my joys and of your own.

4 Lord, with these prospects full in sight,
I'll wait thy signal for my flight;
For, while thy service I pursue,
I find my heaven begun below.

OLD ELTHAM. 7s.

D.C.

194 (884) 7s.   Montgomery.

Joining the Church.

PEOPLE of the living God,
   I have sought the world around,
Paths of sin and sorrow trod,
   Peace and comfort nowhere found:
Now to you my spirit turns —
   Turns, a fugitive unblessed:
Brethren, where your altar burns,
   O! receive me into rest.

2 Lonely, I no longer roam,
   Like the cloud, the wind, the wave:
Where you dwell shall be my home,
   Where you die shall be my grave;
Mine the God whom you adore,
   Your Redeemer shall be mine;
Earth can fill my soul no more,
   Every idol I resign.

3 Tell me not of gain or loss,
   Ease, enjoyment, pomp, or power:
Welcome poverty and cross,
   Shame, reproach, affliction's hour:
"Follow me:" I know thy voice;
   Jesus, Lord, thy steps I see;
Now I take thy yoke by choice;
   Light thy burden now to me.

195 (879) 7s.   C. Wesley.

Christian Fellowship.

LET us join, ('t is God commands,)
   Let us join our hearts and hands:
Help to gain our calling's hope,
   Build we each the other up:
Still forget the things behind,
   Follow Christ in heart and mind;
Toward the mark unwearied press,
   Seize the crown of righteousness.

2 Plead we thus for faith alone,
   Faith by which our works is shown:
God it is who justifies;
   Only faith the grace applies —
Active faith that lives within;
   Conquers earth, and hell, and sin;
Sanctifies, and makes us whole;
   Forms the Saviour in the soul.

3 Let us for this faith contend;
   Sure salvation is its end;
Heaven already is begun,
   Everlasting life is won.
Only let us persevere,
   Till we see our Lord appear,
Never from the Rock remove,
   Saved by faith, which works by love.

WARWICK. C. M.

196 (923) C. M.   C. WESLEY.

For the Water of Life.

FOUNTAIN of life, to all below
  Let thy salvation roll ;
Water, replenish, and o'erflow,
  Every believing soul.

2 Into that happy number, Lord,
  Us weary sinners take ;
Jesus, fulfil thy gracious word,
  For thine own mercy's sake.

3 Turn back our nature's rapid tide,
  And we shall flow to thee,
While down the stream of time we glide
  To our eternity.

4 The well of life to us thou art,
  Of joy the swelling flood ;
Wafted by thee, with willing heart
  We swift return to God.

5 We soon shall reach the boundless sea,
  Into thy fulness fall ;
Be lost and swallowed up in thee,
  Our God, our all in all.

197 (926) C. M.

" Lighten mine eyes."

O SUN of righteousness, arise
  With healing in thy wing !
To my diseased, my fainting soul,
  Life and salvation bring.

2 These clouds of pride and sin dispel,
  By thine all-piercing beam ;
Lighten mine eyes with faith, my heart
  With holy hope inflame.

3 My mind, by thy all-quick'ning power,
  From low desires set free ;
Unite my scattered thoughts, and fix
  My love entire on thee.

4 Father, thy long-lost son receive ;
  Saviour, thy purchase own ;
Blest Comforter, with peace and joy
  Thy new-made creature crown.

Doxology.

Now let the Father, and the Son,
  And Spirit be adored,
Where there are, works to make him known,
  Or saints to love the Lord.

TELLEMANN. 7s.

198 (937) 7s. NEWTON.

Wrestling.

LORD, I cannot let thee go,
Till a blessing thou bestow:
Do not turn away thy face,
Mine's an urgent, pressing case.

2 Dost thou ask me who I am?
Ah! my Lord, thou know'st my name;
Yet the question gives a plea
To support my suit with thee.

3 Thou didst once a wretch behold,
In rebellion blindly bold,
Scorn thy grace, thy power defy:
That poor rebel, Lord, was I.

4 Once a sinner, near despair,
Sought thy mercy-seat by prayer;
Mercy heard, and set him free:
Lord, that mercy came to me.

5 Many days have passed since then,
Many changes I have seen;
Yet have been upheld till now!
Who could hold me up but thou?

6 Thou hast helped in every need;
This emboldens me to plead:
After so much mercy past,
Canst thou let me sink at last?

7*

7 No; I must maintain my hold,
'T is thy goodness makes me bold;
I can no denial take,
When I plead for Jesus' sake.

199 (572) 7s. C. WESLEY.

Persevering Grace.

SON of God, thy blessing grant;
Still supply our every want!
Tree of life, thy influence shed!
With thy sap my spirit feed.

2 Tenderest branch, alas! am I,
Wither without thee and die;
Weak as helpless infancy;
O confirm my soul in thee!

3 Unsustained by thee I fall;
Send the help for which I call:
Weaker than a bruised reed,
Help I every moment need.

4 All my hopes on thee depend;
Love me, save me to the end:
Give me the continuing grace,
Take the everlasting praise.

NORTHFIELD. C. M.

Above the moun-

Behold, the mountain of the Lord In latter days shall rise Above the mountains and the hills,

tains and the hills, And draw the wond'ring eyes.

Above the mountains and the hills, And draw the won-d'ring eyes.
Above the mountains and the hills,

200 (456) C. M.   C. WESLEY.

Opening Worship.

O FOR a thousand tongues to sing
  My great Redeemer's praise!
The glories of my God and King,
The triumphs of his grace!

2 My gracious Master and my God,
  Assist me to proclaim, —
To spread through all the earth abroad
  The honors of thy Name.

3 Jesus! the Name that charms our fears,
  That bids our sorrows cease;
'T is music in the sinner's ears,
  'T is life, and health, and peace.

4 He breaks the power of cancelled sin,
  He sets the pris'ner free:
His blood can make the foulest clean:
  His blood availed for me.

201 (562) C. M.   WATTS.

Psalm lxxi. 15.

MY Saviour, my almighty Friend,
  When I begin thy praise,
Where will the growing numbers end,
The numbers of thy grace?

2 Thou art my everlasting trust;
  Thy goodness I adore;
Send down thy grace, O blessed Lord,
That I may love thee more.

3 My feet shall travel all the length
  Of the celestial road;
And march with courage in thy strength,
To see the Lord my God.

4 Awake! awake! my tuneful powers:
  With this delightful song
I'll entertain the darkest hours,
Nor think the season long.

202 (460) L. M. J. WESLEY.

[From the German of Zinzendorf.]

Receiving the Atonement.

JESUS, thy blood and righteousness
My beauty are, my glorious dress:
'Midst flaming worlds, in these arrayed,
With joy shall I lift up my head.

2 Bold shall I stand in thy great day,
For who aught to my charge shall lay?
Fully absolved through these I am,
From sin and fear, from guilt and shame.

3 The holy, meek, unspotted Lamb,
Who from the Father's bosom came,
Who died for me, e'en me, t' atone,
Now for my Lord and God I own.

4 Lord, I believe thy precious blood,
Which, at the mercy-seat of God,
For ever doth for sinners plead,
For *me*, e'en for *my* soul, was shed.

5 Lord, I believe were sinners more
Than sands upon the ocean shore,
Thou hast for ALL a ransom paid,
For ALL a full atonement made.

203 (465) S. M. WATTS.

Adoption.

BEHOLD! what wondrous grace
The Father hath bestowed
On sinners of a mortal race,—
To call them sons of God!

2 'T is no surprising thing
That we should be unknown:
The Jewish world knew not their King,
God's everlasting Son.

3 Nor does it yet appear
How great we must be made;
But when we see our Saviour here,
We shall be like our Head.

4 A hope so much divine,
May trials well endure,
May purge our souls from sense and sin,
As Christ, the Lord, is pure.

5 If in my Father's love
I share a filial part,
Send down thy Spirit, like a dove,
To rest upon my heart.

204 (474) C. M. WATTS.

The Transports of Love.

O 'T IS delight without alloy,
Jesus, to hear thy name:
My spirit leaps with inward joy,
I feel the sacred flame.

2 My passions hold a pleasing reign,
When love inspires my breast,
Love, the divinest of the train,
The sovereign of the rest.

3 This is the grace must live and sing
When faith and hope shall cease,
Must sound from every joyful string
Through the sweet groves of bliss.

4 Let life immortal seize my clay:
Let love refine my blood;
Her flames can bear my soul away,
Can bring me near my God.

5 Swift I ascend the heavenly place,
And hasten to my home:
I leap to meet thy kind embrace,
I come, O Lord, I come!

205 (493) S. M. C. WESLEY.

The New Creation.

THE thing my God doth hate,
That I no more may do,
Thy creature, Lord, again create,
And all my soul renew:
My soul shall then, like thine,
Abhor the thing unclean,
And, sanctified by love divine,
For ever cease from sin.

2 That blessed law of thine,
Jesus, to me impart,
The Spirit's law of life divine,
O write it in my heart!
Implant it deep within,
Whence it may ne'er remove,
The law of liberty from sin,
The perfect law of love.

3 Thy nature be my law,
Thy spotless sanctity:
And sweetly every moment draw
My happy soul to thee.
Soul of my soul remain!
Who didst for all fulfil,
In me, O Lord, fulfil again
Thy Heavenly Father's will!

MONMOUTH. L. M.

206 (461) L. M.   C. WESLEY.
The Work of Faith.

AUTHOR of faith, eternal Word,
    Whose Spirit breathes the active
      flame,
Faith, like its Finisher and Lord,
To-day, as yesterday, the same:

2 To thee our humble hearts aspire,
    And ask the gift unspeakable:
Increase in us the kindled fire,
    In us the work of faith fulfil.

3 By faith we know thee strong to save:
    (Save us, a present Saviour, thou!)
Whate'er we hope, by faith we have;
    Future and past subsisting now.

4 To him that in thy name believes,
    Eternal life with thee is given:
Into himself he all receives,—
    Pardon, and holiness, and heaven.

5 The things unknown to feeble sense,
    Unseen by reason's glimm'ring ray,
With strong, commanding evidence,
    Their heavenly origin display.

207 (510) L. M.   C. WESLEY.
The Believer's Rest.

COME, O thou greater than our heart,
    And make thy faithful mercies
      known:
The mind which was in thee impart;
    Thy constant mind in us be shown.

2 O let us by thy cross abide,
    Thee, only thee, resolved to know,—
The Lamb for sinners crucified,
    A world to save from endless woe.

3 Take us into thy people's rest,
    And we from our own works shall cease:
With thy meek spirit arm our breast,
    And keep our minds in perfect peace.

4 Jesus, for this we calmly wait:
    O let our eyes behold thee near!
Hasten to make our heaven complete,
    Appear, our glorious God, appear!

208 (463) S. M.   WATTS.

Psalm xxxii. 1–6.

O BLESSED souls are they,
 Whose sins are covered o'er!
Divinely blessed, to whom the Lord
Imputes their guilt no more.

2 They mourn their follies past,
 And keep their hearts with care:
Their lips and lives, without deceit,
Shall prove their faith sincere.

3 While I concealed my guilt,
 I felt the fest'ring wound;
Till I confessed my sins to thee,
And ready pardon found.

4 Let sinners learn to pray,
 Let saints keep near the throne:
Our help in times of deep distress
Is found in God alone.

209 (480) L. M.   C. WESLEY.

Proverbs iii. 13–18.

HAPPY the man that finds the grace,
 The blessing of God's chosen race,
The wisdom coming from above,
The faith that sweetly works by love.

2 Happy, beyond description, he
Who knows " the Saviour died for me!"
The gift unspeakable obtains,
And heavenly understanding gains.

3 Wisdom Divine! who tells the price
Of wisdom's costly merchandise?
Wisdom to silver we prefer.
And gold is dross compared to her.

4 Her hands are filled with length of days,
True riches and immortal praise —
Riches of Christ on all bestowed,
And honor that descends from God.

210 (483) 11s & 9s.   C. WESLEY.

Ecstasy of the New-Born Soul.

HOW happy are they Who their
 Saviour obey,
And have laid up their treasures above!
Tongue cannot express The sweet com-
 fort and peace
Of a soul in its earliest love!

2 That comfort was mine, When the favor
 divine,
I first found in the blood of the Lamb:
When my heart it believed, What a joy
 I received,
What a heaven in Jesus' name!

3 'T was a heaven below My Redeemer to
 know,
And the angels could do nothing more
Than fall at his feet, And the story
 repeat,
And the Lover of sinners adore.

4 Jesus all the day long Was my joy and
 my song:
O that all his salvation might see!
He hath loved me, I cried, He hath
 suffered and died,
To redeem a poor rebel like me.

5 On the wings of his love I was carried
 above
All sin, and temptation, and pain:
I could not believe That I ever should
 grieve,
That I ever should suffer again.

6 I rode on the sky, Freely justified I,
Nor did envy Elijah his seat:
My soul mounted higher In a chariot of
 fire,
And the moon it was under my feet.

7 O the rapturous height Of that holy de-
 light
Which I felt in the life-giving blood!
Of my Saviour possessed, I was perfectly
 blessed
As if filled with the fulness of God.

F

211 (469) 8s & 6s.   C. WESLEY.
" *Whereby we cry, Abba, Father.*"

ARISE, my soul, arise,
    Shake off thy guilty fears,
The bleeding Sacrifice
    In my behalf appears:
Before the throne my Surety stands,
My name is written on his hands.

2 He ever lives above,
    For me to intercede;
His all-redeeming love,
    His precious blood to plead:
His blood atoned for all our race,
And sprinkles now the throne of grace.

3 Five bleeding wounds he bears,
    Received on Calvary;
They pour effectual prayers,
    They strongly speak for me:
" Forgive him, O forgive," they cry,
" Nor let that ransomed sinner die!"

4 The Father hears him pray,
    His dear Anointed One:
He cannot turn away
    The presence of his Son:
His Spirit answers to the blood,
And tells me I am born of God.

5 My God is reconciled,
    His pard'ning voice I hear:
He owns me for his child,
    I can no longer fear:
With confidence I now draw nigh,
And Father, Abba, Father, cry.

212 (514) 6s & 8s.   C. WESLEY.
Rejoicing in Hope.

YE ransomed sinners, hear,
    The pris'ners of the Lord,
And wait till Christ appear,
    According to his word:
Rejoice in hope, rejoice with me,
We shall from all our sins be free.

2 In God we put our trust;
    If we our sins confess,
Faithful is he, and just,
    From all unrighteousness
To cleanse us all, both you and me:
We shall from all our sins be free.

3 The word of God is sure,
    And never can remove;
We shall in heart be pure,
    And perfected in love:
Rejoice in hope, rejoice with me,
We shall from all our sins be free.

4 Then let us gladly bring
    Our sacrifice of praise:
Let us give thanks and sing,
    And glory in his grace:
Rejoice in hope, rejoice with me,
We shall from all our sins be free.

213 (473) 7s.   COWPER.
Love to the Saviour.

HARK, my soul, it is the Lord!
    'Tis thy Saviour, hear his word!
Jesus speaks, he speaks to thee:
" Say, poor sinner, lov'st thou me.

2 " I delivered thee when bound,
And, when bleeding, healed thy wound:
Sought thee wand'ring, set thee right,
Turned thy darkness into light.

3 " Can a mother's tender care,
Cease toward the child she bare?
Yes, she may forgetful be,
Yet will I remember thee.

4 " Mine is an unchanging love,
Higher than the heights above,
Deeper than the depths beneath,
Free and faithful, strong as death.

5 " Thou shalt see my glory soon,
When the work of faith is done,
Partner of my throne shalt be:
Say, poor sinner, lov'st thou me?"

6 Lord, it is my chief complaint
That my love is still so faint;
Yet I love thee and adore:
O for grace to love thee more?

214 (476) C. M.   J. NEWTON.

" The fruit of the Spirit is — joy."

JOY is a fruit that will not grow
  In nature's barren soil;
All we can boast, till Christ we know,
  Is vanity and toil.

2 But where the Lord has planted grace,
  And made his glories known,
There fruits of heavenly joy and peace
  Are found — and there alone.

3 A bleeding Saviour seen by faith —
  A sense of pard'ning love —
A hope that triumphs over death —
  Give joys like those above.

4 To take a glimpse within the veil —
  To know that God is mine —
Are springs of joy that never fail,
  Unspeakable, divine!

5 These are the joys which satisfy,
  And sanctify the mind;
Which make the spirit mount on high,
  And leave the world behind.

215 (478) L. M.   J. WESLEY.

Love and Joy.

HOW can it be, thou heavenly King,
  That thou shouldst us to glory
    bring?
Make slaves the partners of thy throne,
Decked with a never-fading crown!

2 Hence our hearts melt, our eyes o'erflow,
Our words are lost, nor will we know —
Nor will we think of aught beside,
" My Lord, my Love is crucified."

3 Ah! Lord, enlarge our scanty thought,
To know the wonders thou hast wrought;
Unloose our stamm'ring tongues to tell
Thy love immense, unsearchable!

4 First-born of many brethren thou,
To thee, lo, all our souls we bow:
To thee our hearts and hands we give,
Thine may we die, thine may we live.

216 (481) C. M.   WATTS.

Rejoicing in God.

MY God, the spring of all my joys,
  The life of my delights,
The glory of my brightest days,
  And comfort of my nights!

2 In darkest shades, if thou appear,
  My dawning is begun:
Thou art my soul's bright morning star,
  And thou my rising sun.

3 The opening heavens around me shine
  With beams of sacred bliss,
If Jesus show his mercy mine,
  And whisper I am his.

4 My soul would leave this heavy clay
  At that transporting word,
Run up with joy the shining way,
  To see and praise my Lord.

5 Fearless of hell and ghastly death,
  I'd break through every foe:
The wings of love and arms of faith
  Would bear me conqueror through.

217 (506) C. M.   C. WESLEY.

" Thy will be done."

JESUS, the life, the truth, the way,
  In whom I now believe,
As taught by thee, in faith I pray,
  Expecting to receive.

2 Thy will by me on earth be done,
  As by the powers above,
Who always see thee on thy throne,
  And glory in thy love.

3 I ask in confidence the grace,
  That I may do thy will,
As angels who behold thy face,
  And all thy words fulfil.

4 Surely I shall, the sinner I,
  Shall serve thee without fear,
If thou my nature sanctify
  In answer to my prayer.

STEPHENS. C. M.

W. JONES.

218 (504) C. M.   C. WESLEY.

Cordial Obedience.

COME, Lord, and claim me for thine
    own,
Saviour, thy right assert!
Come, gracious Lord, set up thy throne,
And reign within my heart!

2 The day of thy great power I feel,
    And pant for liberty;
I loathe myself, deny my will,
    And give up all for thee.

3 I hate my sins, no longer mine,
    For I renounce them too;
My weakness with thy strength I join,
    Thy strength shall all subdue.

4 So shall I bless thy pleasing sway
    And, sitting at thy feet,
Thy laws with all my heart obey,
    With all my soul submit.

5 Thy love the conquest more than gains,
    To all I shall proclaim,
Jesus, the King, the Conqu'ror, reigns,
    Bow down to Jesus' name.

219 (500) C. M.   C. WESLEY.

The Rapture of Love.

I KNOW that my Redeemer lives,
    And ever prays for me;
A token of his love he gives,
    A pledge of liberty.

2 I find him lifting up my head,
    He brings salvation near:
His presence makes me free indeed,
    And he will soon appear.

3 He wills that I should holy be!
    What can withstand his will?
The counsel of his grace in me
    He surely shall fulfil.

4 Jesus, I hang upon thy word;
    I steadfastly believe
Thou wilt return, and claim me, Lord,
    And to thyself receive.

5 Joyful in hope, my spirit soars
    To meet thee from above,
Thy goodness thankfully adores;
    And sure I taste thy love.

220 (505)C. M.   C. WESLEY.

A Holy Heart, the Saviour's Home.

WHAT is our calling's glorious hope
   But inward holiness?
For this to Jesus I look up,
   I calmly wait for this.

2 I wait, till he shall touch me clean,
   Shall life and power impart,
Give me the faith that casts out sin,
   And purifies the heart.

3 This is the dear redeeming grace,
   For every sinner free:
Surely it shall on me take place,
   The chief of sinners, me.

4 From all iniquity, from all,
   He shall my soul redeem!
In Jesus I believe, and shall
   Believe myself to him.

5 When Jesus makes my heart his home,
   My sin shall all depart;
And, lo! he saith, "I quickly come,
   To fill and rule thy heart!"

6 Be it according to thy word,
   Redeem me from all sin:
My heart would now receive thee, Lord;
   Come in, my Lord, come in!

221 (512) C. M.   C. WESLEY.

Rejoicing in Hope.

O JOYFUL sound of gospel grace!
   Christ shall in me appear:
I, even I, shall see his face;
   I shall be holy here.

2 The glorious crown of righteousness
   To me reached out I view;
Conqu'ror through him, I soon shall
     seize,
   And wear it as my due.

3 The promised land from Pisgah's top
   I now exult to see:
My hope is full (O glorious hope!)
   Of immortality.

4 He visits now the house of clay;
   He shakes his future home:
O wouldst thou, Lord, on this glad day,
   Into thy temple come!

8

222 (538) L. M.   C. WESLEY.

Seeking Perfect Rest in Christ.

O THAT my load of sin were gone!
   O that I could at last submit
At Jesus' feet to lay it down!
   To lay my soul at Jesus' feet!

2 Rest for my soul I long to find:
   Saviour of all, if mine thou art,
Give me thy meek and lowly mind,
   And stamp thine image on my heart.

3 Break off the yoke of inbred sin,
   And fully set my spirit free:
I cannot rest till pure within,
   Till I am wholly lost in thee.

4 Fain would I learn of thee, my God,
   Thy light and easy burden prove,
The cross, all stained with hallowed
     blood,
   The labor of thy dying love.

5 I would, but thou must give the power;
   My heart from every sin release;
Bring near, bring near the joyful hour,
   And fill me with thy perfect peace.

6 Come, Lord, the drooping sinner cheer,
   Nor let thy chariot wheels delay:
Appear, in my poor heart appear!
   My God, my Saviour, come away!

223 (544)C. M.   C. WESLEY.

Seeking a Perfect Cure.

DEEPEN the wound thy hands have
     made
In this weak, helpless soul,
Till mercy, with its balmy aid,
Descend to make me whole.

2 The sharpness of thy two-edged sword
   Enable me t' endure;
Till bold to say, My hallowing Lord
   Hath wrought a perfect cure.

3 I see th' exceeding broad command,
   Which all contains in one;
Enlarge my heart to understand
   The mystery unknown.

4 O that with all thy saints I might
   By sweet experience prove
What is the length, and breadth, and
     height,
   And depth, of perfect love!

CHIMES. C. M.

224 (498) C. M.   C. WESLEY.

The Rest of Faith.

I WOULD be thine, thou know'st I
    would,
And have thee all my own;
Thee, O my all-sufficient Good!
    I want, and thee alone.

2 Thy name to me, thy nature grant!
    This, only this, be given:
Nothing besides my God I want;
    Nothing in earth or heaven.

3 Come, O my Saviour, come away!
    Into my soul descend!
No longer from thy creature stay,
    My Author and my End!

4 Come, Father, Son, and Holy Ghost
    And seal me thine abode!
Let all I am in thee be lost;
    Let all be lost in God!

225 (528) C. M.   C. WESLEY.

The Act of Consecration.

LET Him to whom we now belong
    His sovereign right assert!
And take up every thankful song,
    And every loving heart.

2 He justly claims us for his own,
    Who bought us with a price:
The Christian lives to Christ alone,
    To Christ alone he dies.

3 Jesus, thine own at last receive,
    Fulfil our heart's desire;
And let us to thy glory live,
    And in thy cause expire!

4 Our souls and bodies we resign:
    With joy we render thee
Our all, no longer ours, but thine,
    To all eternity.

EFFINGHAM. L. M.

226 (488) L. M.   Watts.

" Our rejoicing is this " —

LORD, how secure and blessed are they
  Who feel the joys of pardoned sin!
Should storms of wrath shake earth and
    sea,
Their minds have heaven and peace
    within.

2 The day glides sweetly o'er their heads,
  Made up of innocence and love;
And soft and silent as the shades
  Their nightly minutes gently move.

3 Quick as their thoughts their joys come
    on,
  But fly not half so fast away:
Their souls are ever bright as noon,
  And calm as summer evenings be.

4 How oft they look to th' heavenly hills,
  Where groves of living pleasures grow!
And longing hopes and cheerful smiles
  Sit undisturbed upon their brow.

227 (477) L. M.

Love and Joy.

I THIRST, thou wounded Lamb of God,
  To wash me in thy cleansing blood;
To dwell within thy wounds: then pain
Is sweet, and life or death is gain.

2 Take my poor heart, and let it be
For ever closed to all but thee!
Seal thou my breast, and let me wear
That pledge of love for ever there.

3 How blessed are they who still abide
Close sheltered in thy bleeding side!
Who life and strength from thence de-
    rive,
And by thee move, and in thee live.

4 What are our works but sin and death,
Till thou thy quick'ning Spirit breathe?
Thou giv'st the power thy grace to
    move,
O wondrous grace! O boundless love!

228 **(555)** S. M.   C. WESLEY.

Strangers and Pilgrims.

IN every time and place,
  Who serve the Lord most high,
Are called his sovereign will t' embrace,
  And still their own deny,—

2 To follow his command
  On earth as pilgrims rove,
And seek an undiscovered land,
  And house and friends above.

3 Father, the narrow path
  To that far country show;
And in the steps of Abrah'm's faith
  Enable me to go.

4 A cheerful sojourner
  Where'er thou bidd'st me roam,
Till, guided by thy Spirit here,
  I reach my heavenly home.

229 **(565)** C. M.   DODDRIDGE.

" And Enoch walked with God."

CHEERED with thy converse, Lord, I
  trace
  The desert with delight;
Through all the gloom, one smile of thine
  Can dissipate the night.

2 Nor shall I through eternal days
  A restless pilgrim roam;
Thy hand, that now directs my course,
  Shall soon convey me home.

3 I ask not Enoch's rapt'rous flight
  To realms of heavenly day;
Nor seek Elijah's fiery steeds,
  To bear this flesh away.

4 Joyful my spirit will consent
  To drop its mortal load;
And hail the sharpest pangs of death,
  That break its way to God.

230 **(566)** L. M.   WATTS.

The Christian Race.

AWAKE, our souls! away, our fears!
  Let every trembling thought be
  gone!
Awake, and run the heavenly race,
  And put a cheerful courage on.

2 True, 't is a strait and thorny road,
  And mortal spirits tire and faint;
But they forget the mighty God
  That feeds the strength of every saint.

3 From him, the overflowing spring,
  Our souls shall drink a fresh supply;
While such as trust their native strength,
  Shall melt away, and droop, and die.

231 **(611)** C. M.   C. WESLEY.

Judges v. 31.

JESUS, let all thy lovers shine,
  Illustrious as the sun:
And, bright with borrowed rays divine,
  Their glorious circuit run.

2 Beyond the reach of mortals, spread
  Their light where'er they go;
And heavenly influences shed
  On all the world below.

3 As giants may they run their race,
  Exulting in their might;
As burning luminaries, chase
  The gloom of hellish night.

4 As the bright Sun of righteousness,
  Their healing wings display;
And let their lustre still increase
  Unto the perfect day.

232 **(613)** L. M.   GRIGG.

Not Ashamed of Jesus.

JESUS! and shall it ever be
  A mortal man ashamed of thee?
Ashamed of thee, whom angels praise,
Whose glories shine through endless
  days?

2 Ashamed of Jesus! sooner far
  Let evening blush to own a star:
He sheds the beams of light divine
  O'er this benighted soul of mine.

3 Ashamed of Jesus! just as soon
  Let midnight be ashamed of noon:
'T is midnight with my soul, till he,
Bright Morning Star, bid darkness flee!

4 Ashamed of Jesus! that dear Friend
  On whom my hopes of heaven depend?
No: when I blush, be this my shame,
That I no more revere his name.

PETERBORO'. C. M.

233 (497) C. M.   C. WESLEY.
The Rest of Faith.

LORD, I believe a rest remains,
  To all thy people known;
A rest where pure enjoyment reigns,
· And thou art loved alone:

2 A rest where all our soul's desire
  Is fixed on things above;
Where fear, and sin, and grief expire,
  Cast out by perfect love.

3 O that I now the rest might know,
  Believe, and enter in!
Now, Saviour, now the power bestow,
  And let me cease from sin!

4 Remove this hardness from my heart,
  This unbelief remove:
To me the rest of faith impart,
  The Sabbath of thy love.

234 (503) C. M.   C. WESLEY.
The Paradise of Love.

O JESUS! at thy feet we wait,
  Till thou shalt bid us rise,
Restored to our unsinning state,
  To love's sweet paradise.

8 *

2 Saviour from sin, we thee receive,
  From all indwelling sin:
Thy blood, we steadfastly believe,
  Shall make us throughly clean.

3 Since thou wouldst have us free from sin,
  And pure as those above,
Make haste to bring thy nature in,
  And perfect us in love!

235 (494) C. M.   C. WESLEY.
Perfect Purification.

FOR ever here my rest shall be,
  Close to thy bleeding side;
This all my hope, and all my plea,
  For me the Saviour died.

2 My dying Saviour, and my God,
  Fountain for guilt and sin,
Sprinkle me ever with thy blood,
  And cleanse and keep me clean.

3 Wash me, and make me thus thine own;
  Wash me, and mine thou art;
Wash me, but not my feet alone,
  My hands, my head, my heart.

4 Th' atonement of thy blood apply,
  Till faith to sight improve,
Till hope in full fruition die,
  And all my soul be love.

WEBER. 7s.

236 (536) 7s.   J. WESLEY.

[From the German of Schindler.]

Panting for Purity.

HOLY Lamb, who thee receive,
  Who in thee begin to live,
Day and night they cry to thee,
As thou art, so let us be!

2 Jesus, see my panting breast!
See I pant in thee to rest!
Gladly would I now be clean;
Cleanse me now from every sin.

3 Fix, O fix my wav'ring mind!
To thy cross my spirit bind:
Earthly passions far remove;
Swallow up my soul in love.

4 Dust and ashes though we be,
Full of sin and misery,
Thine we are, thou Son of God:
Take the purchase of thy blood!

5 See, ye sinners, see the flame,
Rising from the slaughtered Lamb,
Marks the new, the living way,
Leading to eternal day.

237 (542) 7s.   C. WESLEY.

Longing to be Complete in Christ.

SAVIOUR of the sin-sick soul,
  Give me faith to make me whole:
Finish thy great work of grace;
Cut it short in righteousness.

2 Speak the second time, "Be clean!"
Take away my inbred sin:
Every stumbling-block remove;
Cast it out by perfect love.

3 Nothing less will I require,
Nothing more can I desire:
None but Christ to me be given;
None but Christ in earth or heaven.

4 O that I might now decrease!
O that all I am might cease!
Let me into nothing fall!
Let my Lord be all in all!

Doxology.

Sing we to our God above,
Praise eternal as his love;
Praise him, all ye heavenly host—
Father, Son, and Holy Ghost.

DENNIS. S. M.

NAGELI.

238 (546) S. M.   C. WESLEY.
Waiting at the Cross.

FATHER, I dare believe
Thee merciful and true:
Thou wilt my guilty soul forgive,
My fallen soul renew.

2 Come, then, for Jesus' sake,
And bid my heart be clean:
An end of all my troubles make,
An end of all my sin.

3 I cannot wash my heart,
But by believing thee,
And waiting for thy blood t' impart
The spotless purity.

4 While at thy cross I lie,
Jesus, the grace bestow;
Now thy all-cleansing blood apply,
And I am white as snow.

239 (466) S. M.   C. WESLEY.
Witness of Adoption.

HOW can a sinner know
His sins on earth forgiven?
How can my gracious Saviour show
My name inscribed in heaven!

2 What we have felt and seen
With confidence we tell;
And publish to the sons of men
The signs infallible.

3 We who in Christ believe
That he for us hath died,
We all his unknown peace receive,
And feel his blood applied.

4 Exults our rising soul,
Disburdened of her load,
And swells unutterably full
Of glory and of God.

240 (467) S. M.   C. WESLEY.
Witness of Adoption.

WE by his Spirit prove,
And know the things of God,
The things which freely of his love
He hath on us bestowed.

2 His Spirit us he gave,
Who dwells in us, we know:
The witness in ourselves we have,
And all its fruits we show.

3 The meek and lowly heart
That in our Saviour was,
To us his Spirit does impart,
And signs us with his cross.

4 Our nature's turned, our mind
Transformed in all its powers;
And both the witnesses are joined,
The Spirit of God with ours.

241 **(217)** S. M.   C. WESLEY.
Work and Witness.

O COME, and dwell in me,
  Spirit of power within!
And bring the glorious liberty
From sorrow, fear, and sin.

2 This inward, dire disease,
  Spirit of health, remove,
Spirit of finished holiness,
Spirit of perfect love.

3 Hasten the joyful day
  Which shall my sins consume,
When old things shall be done away,
And all things new become.

4 I want the witness, Lord,
  That all I do is right,
According to thy will and word,
Well pleasing in thy sight.

5 I ask no higher state;
  Indulge me but in this;
And soon or later then translate
To my eternal bliss.

242 **(541)** . C. M.   C. WESLEY.
Longing to be Established in Love.

O THAT in me the sacred fire
  Might now begin to glow!
Burn up the dross of base desire,
And make the mountains flow!

2 O that it now from heaven might fall,
  And all my sins consume!
Come, Holy Ghost, for thee I call,
Spirit of burning, come!

3 Refining fire, go through my heart,
  Illuminate my soul;
Scatter thy life through every part,
And sanctify the whole.

4 No longer then my heart shall mourn,
  While, purified by grace,
I only for his glory burn,
And always see his face.

243 **(577)** S. M.   C. WESLEY.
Depending on Christ.

STILL stir me up to strive
  With thee in strength divine;
And every moment, Lord, revive
This fainting soul of mine.

2 Persist to save my soul
  Throughout the fiery hour,
Till I am every whit made whole,
And show forth all thy power.

3 Through fire and water bring
  Into the wealthy place;
And teach me the new song to sing,
When perfected in grace!

4 O make me all like thee,
  Before I hence remove!
Settle, confirm, and stablish me,
And build me up in love.

5 Let me thy witness live,
  When sin is all destroyed;
And then my spotless soul receive,
And take me home to God.

244 **(587)** S. M.   C. WESLEY.
Watchfulness.

THOU seest my feebleness:
  Jesus, be thou my power,
My help and refuge in distress,
My fortress and my tower.

2 Give me to trust in thee;
  Be thou my sure abode:
My horn, and rock, and buckler be,
My Saviour, and my God.

3 Myself I cannot save,
  Myself I cannot keep;
But strength in thee I surely have
Whose eyelids never sleep.

4 My soul to thee alone,
  Now, therefore, I commend:
Thou, Jesus, love me as thine own,
And love me to the end!

AVON. C. M.

SCOTTISH.

245 (533) C. M.   C. WESLEY.

Praying for a Holy Heart.

O FOR a heart to praise my God,
    A heart from sin set free!
A heart that always feels thy blood
So freely spilt for me!—

2 A heart resigned, submissive, meek,
    My great Redeemer's throne,—
Where only Christ is heard to speak,
Where Jesus reigns alone.

3 O for a lowly, contrite heart,
    Believing, true, and clean!
Which neither life nor death can part
From Him that dwells within:

4 A heart in every thought renewed,
    And full of love divine;
Perfect, and right, and pure, and good,—
A copy, Lord, of thine.

Doxology.

Now let the Father, and the Son,
    And Spirit be adored,   [known,
Where there are works to make him
    Or saints to love the Lord.

246 (540) C. M.   C. WESLEY.

Longing to be Established in Love.

MY God! I know, I feel thee mine,
    And will not quit my claim,
Till all I have is lost in thine,
And all renewed I am.

2 I hold thee with a trembling hand,
    But will not let thee go,
Till steadfastly by faith I stand,
And all thy goodness know.

3 When shall I see the welcome hour
    That plants my God in me!
Spirit of health, and life, and power,
    And perfect liberty!

4 Jesus, thine all-victorious love
    Shed in my heart abroad;
Then shall my feet no longer rove,
    Rooted and fixed in God.

Doxology.

Now let the Father, and the Son,
    And Spirit be adored,   [known,
Where there are works to make him
    Or saints to love the Lord.

TAMWORTH. 8s, 7s, & 4s. LOCKHART.

247 (558) 7s. W. WILLIAMS.
The Pilgrimage.

GUIDE me, O thou great Jehovah,
  Pilgrim through this barren land;
I am weak, but thou art mighty;
  Hold me with thy powerful hand:
    Bread of heaven,
  Feed me till I want no more.

2 Open, Lord, the crystal fountain
  Whence the healing waters flow;
Let the fiery, cloudy pillar,
  Lead me all my journey through:
    Strong Deliv'rer!
  Be thou still my strength and shield.

3 When I tread the verge of Jordan,
  Bid my anxious fears subside;
Death of death, and hell's destruction,
  Land me safe on Canaan's side:
    Songs of praises
  I will ever give to thee.

248 (471) 8s, 7s & 4s.
" Whom not having seen, we love."

O THOU God of my salvation,
  My Redeemer from all sin,
Moved by thy divine compassion,
  Who has died my heart to win,
    I will praise thee;
  Where will I thy praise begin?

2 Though unseen, I love the Saviour;
  He hath brought salvation near,—
  Manifests his pard'ning favor,
  And when Jesus doth appear,
    Soul and body
  Shall his glorious image bear.

3 While the angel choirs are crying,.
  Glory to the great I AM!
I with them will still be vying,
  Glory! glory to the Lamb!
    O how precious
  Is the sound of Jesus' name!

4 Angels now are hov'ring round us,
  Unperceived they mix the throng,
Wond'ring at the love that crowned us,
  Glad to join the holy song:
    Hallelujah!
  Love and praise to Christ belong.

5 Now I see with joy and wonder,
  Whence the gracious spring arose;
Angel minds are lost to ponder
  Dying love's mysterious cause:
    Yet the blessing
  Down to all, to me it flows.

AMSTERDAM. 7s & 6s. DR. NARES.

249 (556) 7s & 6s.   SEAGRAVE.
The Pilgrimage.

RISE, my soul, and stretch thy wings,
  Thy better portion trace;
Rise from transitory things,
  Toward heaven, thy native place:
Sun, and moon, and stars decay;
  Time shall soon this earth remove:
Rise, my soul, and haste away
  To seats prepared above.

2 Rivers to the ocean run,
  Nor stay in all their course;
Fire ascending seeks the sun:
  Both speed them to their source:
So a soul that 's born of God
  Pants to view his glorious face,
Upward tends to his abode,
  To rest in his embrace.

3 Cease, ye pilgrims, cease to mourn;
  Press onward to the prize;
Soon our Saviour will return,
  Triumphant in the skies.
Yet a season, and you know,
  Happy entrance will be given;
All our sorrows left below,
  And earth exchanged for heaven.

250 (516) 7s & 6s.   C. WESLEY.
Deut. xxxiii. 26–29.
* * * * * * * *

GOD is thine: disdain to fear
  The enemy within:
God shall in thy flesh appear,
  And make an end of sin:
God the man of sin shall slay,
  Fill thee with triumphant joy;
God shall thrust him out, and say,
  " Destroy them all, destroy ! "

4 All the struggle then is o'er,
  And wars and fightings cease:
Israel then shall sin no more,
  But dwell in perfect peace.
All his enemies are gone:
  Sin shall have in him no part:
Israel now shall dwell alone,
  With Jesus in his heart.

5 In a land of corn and wine
  His lot shall be below;
Comforts there, and blessings, join,
  And milk and honey flow:
Jacob's well is in his soul;
  Gracious dew his heavens distil,
Fill his soul, already full,
  And shall for ever fill.

251 (563) C. M.   DODDRIDGE.
Isaiah xxxv. 10.

SING, O ye ransomed of the Lord,
  Your great Deliv'rer sing;
Pilgrims, for Zion's city bound,
  Be joyful in your King.

2 A hand Divine shall lead you on,
  Through all the blissful road,
Till to the sacred mount you rise,
  And see your smiling God.

3 There garlands of immortal joy
  Shall bloom on every head;
While sorrow, sighing, and distress,
  Like shadows, all are fled.

4 March on in your Redeemer's strength,
  Pursue his footsteps still;
And let the prospect cheer your eye,
  While lab'ring up the hill.

252 (561) 7s.   CENNICK.
The Pilgrim's Song.

CHILDREN of the heavenly King,
  As we journey, let us sing;
Sing our Saviour's worthy praise,
Glorious in his works and ways.

2 We are trav'ling home to God,
  In the way our fathers trod;
They are happy now, and we
Soon their happiness shall see.

3 O ye banished seed, be glad!
  Christ our Advocate is made:
Us to save, our flesh assumes,
Brother to our souls becomes.

4 Fear not, brethren, joyful stand
  On the borders of our land;
Jesus Christ, our Father's Son,
Bids us undismayed go on.

5 Lord! obediently we 'll go,
  Gladly leaving all below:
Only thou our leader be,
And we still will follow thee.

253 (564) C. M.   C. WESLEY.
Walking with God.

TALK with us, Lord, thyself reveal,
  While here o'er earth we rove;
Speak to our hearts, and let us feel
  The kindlings of thy love.

2 With thee conversing, we forget
  All time, and toil, and care:
Labor is rest, and pain is sweet,
  If thou, my God, art here.

3 Here then, my God, vouchsafe to stay,
  And bid my heart rejoice;
My bounding heart shall own thy sway,
  And echo to thy voice.

4 Thou callest me to seek thy face;
  'T is all I wish to seek:
T' attend the whispers of thy grace,
  And hear thee inly speak.

5 Let this my every hour employ,
  Till I thy glory see,
Enter into my Master's joy,
  And find my heaven in thee!

254 (568) S. M.   HAMMOND.
The Christian Race.

RACERS of Christ, arise!
  Stand forth, prepare to run!
Toward the goal lift up your eyes,
  And manfully go on.

2 'T is true, the race is sharp;
  But, then, it is not long:
Each racer soon will take his harp,
  And warble Zion's song.

3 Open the eye of faith,
  And view the crown on high;
Break through the snares of sin and
    death;
  To endless glory fly.

4 Nearer approaches make;
  Run to the heavenly land;
The prize of your high calling take
  In your victorious hand.

CHRISTMAS. C. M.

HANDEL.

255 (569) C. M.   WATTS.
Sluggishness Lamented.

MY drowsy powers, why sleep ye so?
Awake, my sluggish soul!
Nothing hath half thy work to do,
Yet nothing's half so dull.

2 Go to the ants; for one poor grain
See how they toil and strive!
Yet we, who have a heaven t' obtain,
How negligent we live!

3 We, for whose sake all nature stands,
And stars their courses move;
We, for whose guard the angel bands
Come flying from above;

4 We, for whom God the Son came down,
And labored for our good :
How careless to secure that crown
He purchased with his blood!

5 Lord, shall we live so sluggish still,
And never act our parts?
Come, Holy Dove, from the heavenly hill
And warm our frozen hearts.

9

256 (567) C. M.   DODDRIDGE.
The Christian Race.

AWAKE, my soul! stretch every nerve,
And press with vigor on :
A heavenly race demands thy zeal,
And an immortal crown.

2 A cloud of witnesses around
Hold thee in full survey :
Forget the steps already trod,
And onward urge thy way.

3 'T is God's all-animating voice
That calls thee from on high
'T is his own hand presents the prize
To thine aspiring eye :

4 That prize, with peerless glories bright,
Which shall new lustre boast,
When victor's wreaths and monarch's
gems
Shall blend in common dust.

5 Blest Saviour! introduced by thee,
Have I my race begun ;
And, crowned with vict'ry, at thy feet
I'll lay my honors down.

G

257 (570) L. M.   J. Wesley.
Zeal Implored.

O THOU who all things canst control,
Chase this dread slumber from my
soul;
With joy and fear, with love and awe,
Give me to keep thy perfect law.

2 O may one beam of thy blest light
Pierce through, dispel, the shade of
night;
Touch my cold breast with heavenly fire,
With holy, conqu'ring zeal inspire.

3 With outstretched hands and streaming
eyes,
Oft I begin to grasp the prize;
I groan, I strive, I watch, I pray:
But ah! how soon it dies away!

4 The deadly slumber soon I feel
Afresh upon my spirit steal:
Rise, Lord, stir up thy quick'ning power,
And wake me, that I sleep no more.

258 (624) S. M.
A Single Eye.

TEACH me, my God and King,
In all things thee to see;
And what I do, in anything,
To do it as for thee; —

2 To scorn the senses' sway,
While still to thee I tend:
In all I do be thou the way,
In all be thou the end.

3 All may of thee partake:
Nothing so small can be,
But draws, when acted for thy sake,
Greatness and worth from thee.

4 If done t' obey thy laws,
E'en servile labors shine:
Hallowed is toil, if this the cause,
The meanest work divine.

5 Thee, then, my God and King,
In all things may I see;
And what I do, in anything,
May it be done for thee!

259 (626) C. M.
"Our good is all divine."

FATHER, to thee my soul I lift;
My soul on thee depends,
Convinced that every perfect gift
From thee alone descends.

2 Mercy and grace are thine alone,
And power and wisdom too:
Without the Spirit of thy Son
We nothing good can do.

3 We cannot speak one useful word,
One holy thought conceive,
Unless, in answer to our Lord,
Thyself the blessing give.

4 His blood demands the purchased grace;
His blood's availing plea
Obtained the help for all our race,
And sends it down to me.

260 (627) C. M.   Doddridge.
The Choice of Moses.

MY soul, with all thy waken'd powers,
Survey the heavenly prize;
Nor let these glittering toys of earth
Allure thy wandering eyes.

2 The splendid crown which Moses sought
Still beams around his brow;
Though soon great Pharaoh's pride
Was taught by death to bow.

3 The joys and treasures of a day
I cheerfully resign;
Rich in that large immortal store,
Secured by grace divine.

4 Let fools my wiser choice deride,
Angels and God approve:
Nor scorn of men, nor rage of hell,
My steadfast soul shall move.

5 With ardent eye, that bright reward
I daily will survey;
And in the blooming prospect lose
The sorrows of the way.

261 (576) S. M.   C. WESLEY.

Depending on Christ.

JESUS, my truth, my way,
  My sure, unerring light,
On thee my feeble steps I stay,
  Which thou wilt guide aright.

2 My wisdom and my guide,
  My counsellor thou art;
O never let me leave thy side,
  Or from thy paths depart!

3 I lift mine eyes to thee,
  Thou gracious bleeding Lamb,
That I may now enlightened be,
  And never put to shame.

4 Never will I remove
  Out of thy hands my cause;
But rest in thy redeeming love,
  And hang upon thy cross.

5 Teach me the happy art,
  In all things to depend
On thee: O never, Lord, depart,
  But love me to the end.

262 (580) 8s & 6s.   C. WESLEY.

Circumspection.

BE it my only wisdom here
  To serve the Lord with filial fear,
With loving gratitude;
Superior sense may I display,
By shunning every evil way,
  And walking in the good.

2 O may I still from sin depart;
A wise and understanding heart,
  Jesus, to me be given!
And let me through thy Spirit know
To glorify my God below,
  And find my way to heaven.

263 (583) L. M.   C. WESLEY.

A Watchful Spirit.

JESUS, my Saviour, Brother, Friend,
  On whom I cast my every care,
On whom for all things I depend,
  Inspire, and then accept my prayer.

2 If I have tasted of thy grace,
  The grace that sure salvation brings;
If with me now thy Spirit stays,
  And, hov'ring, hides me in his wings:

3 Still let him with my weakness stay,
  Nor for a moment's space depart;
Evil and danger turn away,
  And keep till he renews my heart.

4 When to the right or left I stray,
  His voice behind me may I hear,
"Return, and walk in Christ, thy way;
  Fly back to Christ, for sin is near!"

5 Jesus, I fain would walk in thee,
  From nature's every path retreat:
Thou art my way; my leader be,
  And set upon the rock my feet.

264 (586) S. M.   C. WESLEY.

Watchfulness.

GRACIOUS Redeemer, shake
  This slumber from my soul!
Say to me now, "Awake, awake!
  And Christ shall make thee whole."

2 Lay to thy mighty hand;
  Alarm me in this hour;
And make me fully understand
  The thunder of thy power!

3 Give me on thee to call,
  Always to watch and pray,
Lest I into temptation fall,
  And cast my shield away.

4 For each assault prepared
  And ready may I be;
For ever standing on my guard,
  And looking up to thee.

265 (610) S. M.   C. WESLEY.

Putting on the Lord Jesus.

GRACIOUS Redeemer, hear!
   Into my soul come down:
Let it throughout my life appear
   That I have Christ put on.

2 O plant in me thy mind!
   O fix in me thy home!
So shall I cry to all mankind,
   Come to the waters, come!

3 Jesus is full of grace,
   To all his bowels move:
Behold in me, ye fallen race,
   That God is only love.

266 (612) C. M.   DODDRIDGE.

" Thou knowest that I love thee."

DO not I love thee, O my Lord?
   Behold my heart, and see;
And turn each cursed idol out
   That dares to rival thee.

2 Do not I love thee from my soul?
   Then let me nothing love;
Dead be my heart to every joy,
   When Jesus cannot move.

3 Is not thy name melodious still
   To mine attentive ear?
Doth not each pulse with pleasure bound
   My Saviour's voice to hear?

4 Hast thou a lamb in all thy flock
   I would disdain to feed?
Hast thou a foe, before whose face
   I fear thy cause to plead?

5 Would not mine ardent spirit vie
   With angels round the throne,
To execute thy sacred will,
   And make thy glory known?

6 Would not my heart pour forth its blood
   In honor of thy name?

And challenge the cold hand of death
   To damp th' immortal flame?

7 Thou knowest I love thee, dearest Lord;
   But O! I long to soar
Far from the sphere of mortal joys,
   And learn to love thee more.

267 (615) 8s.   NEWTON.

Delight in Christ.

HOW tedious and tasteless the hours
   When Jesus no longer I see!
Sweet prospects, sweet birds, and sweet
    flowers,
   Have all lost their sweetness to me,—
The midsummer sun shines but dim,
   The fields strive in vain to look gay;
But when I am happy in him,
   December's as pleasant as May.

2 His name yields the richest perfume,
   And sweeter than music his voice;
His presence disperses my gloom,
   And makes all within me rejoice:
I should, were he always thus nigh,
   Have nothing to wish or to fear;
No mortal so happy as I,
   My summer would last all the year.

3 Content with beholding his face,
   My all to his pleasure resigned;
No changes of season or place
   Would make any change in my mind:
While blessed with a sense of his love,
   A palace a toy would appear;
And prisons would palaces prove,
   If Jesus would dwell with me there.

4 Dear Lord, if indeed I am thine,
   If thou art my sun and my song,
Say why do I languish and pine?
   And why are my winters so long?
O drive these dark clouds from my sky?
   Thy soul-cheering presence restore;
Or take me to thee up on high,
   Where winter and clouds are no more!

MAITLAND. C. M. WESTERN.

268 (616) C. M. WATTS.

" The Lord is my portion."

MY God, my portion, and my love,
My everlasting all,
I've none but thee in heaven above,
Or on this earthly ball.

2 What empty things are all the skies,
And this inferior clod!
There's nothing here deserves my joys,
There's nothing like my God.

3 How vain a toy is glitt'ring wealth,
If once compared to thee:
Or what's my safety, or my health,
Or all my friends, to me?

4 Were I possessor of the earth,
And called the stars my own,
Without thy graces and thyself,
I were a wretch undone.

5 Let others stretch their arms like seas,
And grasp in all the shore:
Grant me the visits of thy face,
And I desire no more.

9 *

269 (619) C. M. WATTS.

Surrendering All for Christ.

HOW vain are all things here below!
How false, and yet how fair!
Each pleasure hath its poison too,
And every sweet a snare.

2 The brightest things below the sky
Give but a flatt'ring light;
We should suspect some danger nigh
Where we possess delight.

3 Our dearest joys and nearest friends,
The partners of our blood,
How they divide our wav'ring minds,
And leave but half for God!

4 The fondness of a creature's love,
How strong it strikes the sense!
Thither the warm affections move,
Nor can we call them thence.

5 Dear Saviour, let thy beauties be
My soul's eternal food;
And grace command my heart away
From all created good.

270 (621) S. M.

Rejoicing in God.

COME, ye that love the Lord,
 And let your joys be known,
Join in a song with sweet accord,
 While ye surround his throne.

2 The sorrows of the mind
 Be banish'd from the place!
Religion never was designed
 To make our pleasures less.

3 Let those refuse to sing,
 Who never knew our God;
But servants of the heavenly King
 May speak their joys abroad.

4 The God that rules on high,
 That all the earth surveys,
That rides upon the stormy sky,
 And calms the roaring seas;

5 This awful God is ours,
 Our Father and our Love;
He will send down his heavenly powers
 To carry us above.

6 There we shall see his face,
 And never, never sin;
There, from the rivers of his grace,
 Drink endless pleasures in:

7 Yea, and before we rise
 To that immortal state,
The thoughts of such amazing bliss
 Should constant joys create.

8 The men of grace have found
 Glory begun below:
Celestial fruit on earthly ground
 From faith and hope may grow.

9 The hill of Zion yields
 A thousand sacred sweets,
Before we reach the heavenly fields,
 Or walk the golden streets.

10 Then let our songs abound,
 And every tear be dry;
We're marching through Immanuel's
 ground
 To fairer worlds on high.

Doxology.

Give to the Father praise;
 Give glory to the Son;
And to the Spirit of his grace
 Be equal honor done.

271 (623) 8s & 7s.

Gratitude.

COME, thou Fount of every blessing,
 Tune my heart to sing thy grace:
Streams of mercy, never ceasing,
 Call for songs of loudest praise,
Teach me some melodious sonnet,
 Sung by flaming tongues above:
Praise the mount — I 'm fixed upon it;
 Mount of thy redeeming love!

2 Here I 'll raise my Ebenezer,
 Hither, by thy help, I 'm come;
And I hope, by thy good pleasure,
 Safely to arrive at home.
Jesus sought me, when a stranger,
 Wand'ring from the fold of God;
He, to rescue me from danger,
 Interposed his precious blood!

3 O! to grace how great a debtor
 Daily I 'm constrained to be!
Let thy goodness, like a fetter,
 Bind my wand'ring heart to thee!
Prone to wander, Lord, I feel it;
 Prone to leave the God I love —
Here 's my heart, O take and seal it!
 Seal it for thy courts above!

Doxology.

Lord, dismiss us with thy blessing,
 Bid us now depart in peace;
Still on heavenly manna feeding,
 Let our faith and love increase:
Fill each breast with consolation;
 Up to thee our hearts we raise:
When we reach our blissful station,
 Then we 'll give thee nobler praise.

272 (628) L. M.   DODDRIDGE.
The Choice of Mary.

BESET with snares on every hand,
  In life's uncertain path I stand:
Saviour divine! diffuse thy light
To guide my doubtful footsteps right.

2 Engage this roving, treach'rous heart
To fix on Mary's better part,
To scorn the trifles of a day,
For joys that none can take away.

3 Then let the wildest storms arise;
Let tempests mingle earth and skies;
No fatal shipwreck shall I fear,
But all my treasures with me bear.

4 If thou, my Jesus, still be nigh,
Cheerful I live, and joyful die;
Secure, when mortal comforts flee,
To find ten thousand worlds in thee.

273 (629) L. M.   J. WESLEY.
Adversity.

O THOU, to whose all-searching sight
  The darkness shineth as the light,
Search, prove my heart, it pants for thee,
O burst these bonds, and set it free!

2 Wash out its stains, refine its dross,
Nail my affections to the cross;
Hallow each thought, let all within
Be clean, as thou, my Lord, art clean.

3 If in this darksome wild I stray,
Be thou my light, be thou my way;
No foes, no violence, I fear,
No fraud, while thou, my God, art near.

4 When rising floods my soul o'erflow,
When sinks my heart in waves of woe,
Jesus, thy timely aid impart,
And raise my head, and cheer my heart.

5 Saviour, where'er thy steps I see,
Dauntless, untired, I follow thee:
O let thy hand support me still,
And lead me to thy holy hill!

6 If rough and thorny be the way,
My strength proportion to my day;
Till toil, and grief, and pain shall cease,
Where all is calm, and joy, and peace.

274 (584) L. M.   C. WESLEY.
A Watchful Spirit.

UPHOLD me, Saviour, or I fall;
  O reach me out thy gracious hand!
Only on thee for help I call;
Only by faith in thee I stand.

2 Pierce, fill me with an humble fear;
My utter helplessness reveal!
Satan and sin are always near,
Thee may I always nearer feel.

3 O that to thee my constant mind
Might with an even flame aspire!
Pride in its earliest motions find
And mark the risings of desire!

4 O that my tender soul might fly
The first abhorred approach of ill:
Quick, as the apple of an eye,
The slightest touch of sin to feel.

275 (638) C. M.
Psalm xxxiv. 1-9.

THROUGH all the changing scenes of
  life,
In trouble and in joy,
The praises of my God shall still
My heart and tongue employ.

2 Of this deliv'rance I will boast,
Till all that are distrest
From my example comfort take,
And charm their griefs to rest.

3 O magnify the Lord with me,
With me exalt his name:
When in distress to him I called,
He to my rescue came.

4 The angel of the Lord encamps
Around the good and just;
Deliv'rance he affords to all
Who on his succor trust.

5 O make but trial of his love,
Experience will decide
How blessed they are, and only they,
Who in his truth confide.

6 Fear him, ye saints; and you will then
Have nothing else to fear:
Make you his service your delight;
Your wants shall be his care.

276 (640) 11s.
Precious Promises.

HOW firm a foundation, ye saints of
the Lord,
Is laid for your faith in his excellent
word!
What more can he say than to you he
hath said,
You who unto Jesus for refuge have fled?

2 In every condition — in sickness, in
health;
In poverty's vale, or abounding in wealth;
At home and abroad; on the land, on
the sea,
"As thy days may demand, shall thy
strength ever be.

3 "Fear not; I am with thee; O be not
dismayed;
I, I am thy God, and will still give thee
aid;
I'll strengthen thee, help thee, and cause
thee to stand,   [hand.
Upheld by my righteous, omnipotent

4 "When through the deep waters I call
thee to go,
The rivers of woe shall not thee overflow;
For I will be with thee thy troubles to
bless,
And sanctify to thee thy deepest distress.

5 "When through fiery trials thy pathway
shall lie,
My grace, all-sufficient, shall be thy
supply:
The flame shall not hurt thee; — I only
design
Thy dross to consume, and thy gold to
refine.

6 "E'en down to old age, all my people
shall prove,
My sovereign, eternal, unchangeable
love;
And when hoary hairs shall their tem-
ples adorn,
Like lambs they shall still in my bosom
be borne.

7 "The soul that on Jesus still leans for
repose,
I *will* not, I *will* not, desert to his foes;
That soul, though all hell should endea-
vor to shake,
I'll *never*, no *never*, no *never* forsake."

277 (632) 8s & 7s.   GRANT.
Taking up the Cross.

JESUS, I my cross have taken,
All to leave and follow thee;
Naked, poor, despised, forsaken,
Thou, from hence, my all shalt be.
Perish, every fond ambition,
All I've sought, or hoped, or known;
Yet how rich is my condition!
God and heaven are still my own!

2 Let the world despise and leave me;
They have left my Saviour too:
Human hearts and looks deceive me —
Thou art not, like them, untrue;
And while thou shalt smile upon me,
God of wisdom, love, and might,
Foes may hate, and friends disown me,
Show thy face, and all is bright.

3 Go, then, earthly fame and treasure;
Come disaster, scorn, and pain;
In thy service pain is pleasure;
With thy favor loss is gain.
I have called thee, Abba, Father,—
I have set my heart on thee:
Storms may howl, and clouds may gather,
All must work for good to me.

4 Man may trouble and distress me,—
'T will but drive me to thy breast;
Life with trials hard may press me,—
Heaven will bring me sweeter rest.
O! 't is not in grief to harm me,
While thy love is left to me!
O! 't were not in joy to charm me,
Were that joy unmixed with thee!

5 Soul, then know thy full salvation;
Rise o'er sin, and fear, and care;
Joy to find in every station
Something still to do or bear.
Think what Spirit dwells within thee;
Think what Father's smiles are thine;
Think that Jesus died to win thee:
Child of heaven, canst thou repine?

6 Haste thee on from grace to glory,
Armed by faith, and winged by prayer;
Heaven's eternal days before thee,
God's own hand shall guide thee there.
Soon shall close thy earthly mission,
Soon shall pass thy pilgrim days;
Hope shall change to glad fruition,
Faith to sight, and prayer to praise.

SILVER STREET. S. M.

SMITH.

278 (643) S. M.   C. WESLEY.

Trust in Providence.

COMMIT thou all thy griefs
  And ways into his hands,
To his sure trust and tender care,
  Who earth and heaven commands:
Who points the clouds their course,
  Whom winds and seas obey,
He shall direct thy wand'ring feet,
  He shall prepare thy way.

2 Thou on the Lord rely,
  So safe shalt thou go on:
Fix on his work thy steadfast eye,
  So shall thy work be done.
No profit canst thou gain
  By self-consuming care;
To him commend thy cause, his ear
  Attends the softest prayer.

3 Thine everlasting truth, —
  Father, thy ceaseless love,
Sees all thy children's wants, and knows
  What best for each will prove;
And whatsoe'er thou will'st,
  Thou dost, O King of kings!
What 's thy unerring wisdom's choice,
  Thy power to being brings!

279 (644) S. M.   J. WESLEY.

Concluded.

GIVE to the winds thy fears;
  Hope, and be undismayed;
God hears thy sighs, and counts thy tears;
  God shall lift up thy head:
Through waves, and clouds, and storms,
  He gently clears thy way;
Wait thou his time, so shall this night
  Soon end in joyous day.

2 Still heavy is thy heart?
  Still sink thy spirits down?
Cast off the weight, let fear depart,
  And every care be gone.
What though thou rulest not,
  Yet heaven, and earth, and hell,
Proclaim, God sitteth on the throne,
  And ruleth all things well.

3 Leave to his sovereign sway,
  To choose and to command;
So shalt thou, wond'ring, own his way,
  How wise, how strong his hand!
Far, far above thy thought
  His counsel shall appear,
When fully he the work hath wrought
  That caused thy needless fear.

280 (642) S. M.　　C. WESLEY.

" All things work together for good."

AWAY! my needless fears,
　And doubts no longer mine;
A ray of heavenly light appears,
　A messenger divine.

2 Thrice comfortable hope,
　That calms my troubled breast;
My Father's hand prepares the cup,
　And what he wills is best.

3 If what I wish is good,
　And suits the will divine, —
By earth and hell in vain withstood,
　I know it shall be mine.

4 Still let them counsel take
　To frustrate his decree;
They cannot keep a blessing back,
　By Heaven designed for me.

5 Here then I doubt no more,
　But in his pleasure rest,
Whose wisdom, love, and truth, and
　power,
Engage to make me blest.

281 (657) S. M.

Eph. vi. 10.

SOLDIERS of Christ, arise!
　And put your armor on,
Strong in the strength which God sup-
　plies
　Through his Eternal Son;
Strong in the Lord of hosts,
　And in his mighty power,
Who in the strength of Jesus trusts
　Is more than conqueror.

2 Stand, then, in his great might,
　With all his strength endued;
But take, to arm you for the fight,
　The panoply of God:
That having all things done,
　And all your conflicts past,
Ye may o'ercome through Christ alone,
　And stand entire at last.

3 From strength to strength go on,
　Wrestle, and fight, and pray:
Tread all the powers of darkness down,
　And win the well-fought day;
Still let the Spirit cry,
　In all his soldiers, "Come,"
Till Christ the Lord descend from high,
　And take the conquerors home.

282 (649) C. M.

Contentment.

MY span of life will soon be done,
　The passing moments say;
As length'ning shadows o'er the mead
　Proclaim the close of day.

2 O that my heart might dwell aloof
　From all created things,
And learn that wisdom from above
　Whence true contentment springs!

3 Courage, my soul, thy bitter cross,
　In every trial here,
Shall bear thee to thy heaven above,
　But shall not enter there.

4 The sighing ones that humbly seek
　In sorrowing paths below,
Shall in eternity rejoice,
　Where endless comforts flow.

5 Soon will the toilsome strife be o'er
　Of sublunary care,
And life's dull vanities no more
　This anxious breast ensnare.

6 Courage, my soul, on God rely,
　Deliv'rance soon will come;
A thousand ways has Providence
　To bring believers home.

283 (651) L. M.

Patience.

THOU Lamb of God, thou Prince of
　peace!
For thee my thirsty soul doth pine;
My longing heart implores thy grace,
O make me in thy likeness shine!

2 With fraudless, even, humble mind,
　Thy will in all things may I see;
In love be every wish resigned,
　And hallowed my whole heart to thee.

3 When pain o'er my weak flesh prevails,
　With lamblike patience arm my breast;
When grief my wounded soul assails,
　In lowly meekness may I rest.

4 Close by thy side still may I keep,
　Howe'er life's various current flow;
With steadfast eye mark every step,
　And follow thee where'er thou go.

LYONS. 5s & 6s.

HAYDN.

284(645) 5s & 6s.

The Lord will Provide.

THOUGH troubles assail,
  And dangers affright,
Though friends should all fail,
  And foes all unite,

2 Yet one thing secures us,
    Whatever betide,
  The promise assures us,
    The Lord will provide.

3 The birds without barn,
    Or storehouse, are fed;
  From them let us learn
    To trust for our bread:

4 His saints what is fitting
    Shall ne'er be denied,
  So long as 't is written,
    The Lord will provide.

5 We all may, like ships,
    By tempests be tost
  On perilous deeps,
    But need not be lost;

6 Though Satan enrages
    The wind and the tide,
  Yet Scripture engages,
    The Lord will provide.

7 His call we obey,
    Like Abrah'm of old:
  We know not the way,
    But faith makes us bold;

8 For though we are strangers,
    We have a sure guide,
  And trust, in all dangers,
    The Lord will provide.

9 No strength of our own,
    Nor goodness we claim,
  Our trust is all thrown
    On Jesus' name;

10 In this our strong tower
     For safety we hide;
   The Lord is our power,
     The Lord will provide.

11 When life sinks apace,
     And death is in view,
   The word of his grace
     Shall comfort us through:

12 Not fearing or doubting,
     With Christ on our side,
   We hope to die shouting,
     The Lord will provide.

HAPPY DAY. C. M.

Hap - py day, hap - py day, When Je - sus washed my sins a - way;

He taught me how to watch and pray, And live re - joic - ing ev - 'ry day.

---

285 (1011) L. M.   DODDRIDGE.

Eucharistic Vow.

O HAPPY day that fixed my choice
   On thee, my Saviour and my God!
Well may this glowing heart rejoice,
   And tell its raptures all abroad.

2 O happy bond, that seals my vows
   To him who merits all my love!
Let cheerful anthems fill his house,
   While to that sacred shrine I move.

3 'Tis done: the great transaction 's done!
   I am my Lord's, and he is mine;
He drew me, and I followed on,
   Charmed to confess the voice divine.

4 Now rest, my long-divided heart;
   Fixed on this blissful centre, rest:
With ashes who would grudge to part,
   When called on angels' bread to feast?

5 High Heaven, that heard the solemn vow,
   That vow renewed shall daily hear,
Till in life's latest hour I bow,
   And bless in death a bond so dear.

---

286 (650) L. M.

Discipline.

MY hope, my all, my Saviour thou,
   To thee, lo, now my soul I bow;
I feel the bliss thy wounds impart,
   I find thee, Saviour, in my heart.

2 Be thou my strength, be thou my way,
   Protect me through my life's short day;
In all my acts may wisdom guide,
   And keep me, Saviour, near thy side.

3 Correct, reprove, and comfort me;
   As I have need, my Saviour be;
And if I would from thee depart,
   Then clasp me, Saviour, to thy heart.

4 In fierce temptation's darkest hour,
   Save me from sin and Satan's power:
Tear every idol from thy throne,
   And reign, my Saviour, reign alone.

5 My suff'ring time shall soon be o'er,
   Then shall I sigh and weep no more;
My ransomed soul shall soar away,
   To sing thy praise in endless day.

287 (194) S. M. DODDRIDGE.

Grace.

GRACE! 'tis a charming sound!
 Harmonious to my ear!
Heaven with the echo shall resound,
And all the earth shall hear.

2 Grace first contrived the way
 To save rebellious man;
And all the steps *that* grace display
 Which drew the wondrous plan.

3 Grace taught my wand'ring feet
 To tread the heavenly road;
And new supplies each hour I meet
 While pressing on to God.

4 Grace all the work shall crown,
 Through everlasting days:
It lays in heaven the topmost stone,
 And well deserves the praise.

288 (654) C. M. NEWTON.

Gratitude and Hope.

AMAZING grace! (how sweet the
 sound!)
That saved a wretch like me!
I once was lost, but now I'm found—
 Was blind, but now I see.

2 'T was grace that taught my heart to fear,
 And grace my fears relieved:
How precious did that grace appear
 The hour I first believed!

3 Through many dangers, toils, and snares
 I have already come:
'T is grace has brought me safe thus far,
 And grace will lead me home.

4 The Lord has promised good to me—
 His word my hope secures:
He will my shield and portion be
 As long as life endures.

5 Yea, when this flesh and heart shall fail,
 And mortal life shall cease,
I shall possess, within the veil,
 A life of joy and peace.

10

289 (655) C. M. WATTS.

Inspiring Hope.

WHEN I can read my title clear
 To mansions in the skies,
I'll bid farewell to every fear,
 And wipe my weeping eyes.

2 Should earth against my soul engage,
 And fiery darts be hurled,
Then I can smile at Satan's rage,
 And face a frowning world.

3 Let cares, like a wild deluge, come,
 Let storms of sorrow fall:
So I but safely reach my home,
 My God, my heaven, my all.

4 There I shall bathe my weary soul
 In seas of heavenly rest,
And not a wave of trouble roll
 Across my peaceful breast.

290 (656) C. M. WATTS.

The Christian Warfare.

AM I a soldier of the cross,—
 A follower of the Lamb,—
And shall I fear to own his cause,
 Or blush to speak his name?

2 Must I be carried to the skies
 On flowery beds of ease,
While others fought to win the prize,
 And sailed through bloody seas?

3 Are there no foes for me to face?
 Must I not stem the flood?
Is this vile world a friend to grace,
 To help me on to God?

4 Sure I must fight if I would reign;
 Increase my courage, Lord:
I'll bear the toil, endure the pain,
 Supported by thy word.

5 Thy saints, in all this glorious war,
 Shall conquer, though they die:
They see the triumph from afar,
 By faith they bring it nigh.

6 When that illustrious day shall rise,
 And all thine armies shine,
In robes of victory, through the skies,
 The glory shall be thine.

HORTON. 7s.

WARTENSEE.

291 (630) 7s.   COWPER.

Chastisement.

'TIS my happiness below,
  Not to live without the cross;
But the Saviour's power to know,
  Sanctifying every loss.

2 Trials must and will befall;
  But with humble faith to see
Love inscribed upon them all,—
  This is happiness to me.

3 Trials make the promise sweet:
  Trials give new life to prayer;
Bring me to my Saviour's feet,
  Lay me low, and keep me there.

292 (502) 7s.

" Christ liveth in me."

LOVING Jesus, gentle Lamb,
  In thy gracious hands I am;
Make me, Saviour, what thou art,
Live thyself within my heart.

2 I shall then show forth thy praise,
  Serve thee all my happy days,
Then the world shall always see
Christ, the holy Child, in me.

293 (551) 7s.   C. WESLEY.

Exulting in Perfect Love.

JESUS, all-atoning Lamb,
  Thine, and only thine, I am:
Take my body, spirit, soul;
Only thou possess the whole.

2 Thou my one thing needful be;
  Let me ever cleave to thee;
Let me choose the better part;
Let me give thee all my heart.

3 Fairer than the sons of men,
  Do not let me turn again,
Leave the fountain-head of bliss,
Stoop to creature happiness.

4 Whom have I on earth below?
  Thee, and only thee, I know:
Whom have I in heaven but thee?
Thou art all in all to me.

5 All my treasure is above;
  All my riches is thy love:
Who the worth of love can tell?
Infinite, unsearchable!

SICILIAN HYMN. 8s & 7s.

294 (479) 8s & 7s.

Sitting at the Cross.

SWEET the moments, rich in blessing,
   Which before the cross I spend;
Life, and health, and peace possessing,
   From the sinner's dying Friend:
Here I'll sit, for ever viewing
   Mercy's streams in streams of blood:
Precious drops, my soul bedewing,
   Plead and claim my peace with God.

2 Truly blessed is this station,
   Low before his cross to lie;
While I see divine compassion
   Floating in his languid eye:
Here it is I find my heaven,
   While upon the Lamb I gaze:
Love I much? I 've much forgiven —
   I 'm a miracle of grace!

3 Love and grief my heart dividing,
   With my tears his feet I 'll bathe;
Constant still in faith abiding,
   Life deriving from his death.
May I still enjoy this feeling,
   In all need to Jesus go;
Prove his wounds each day more healing,
   And himself more deeply know.

295 (239) 8s & 7s.   NEWTON.

Supplies of the Church.

GLORIOUS things of thee are spoken,
   Zion, city of our God!
He, whose word can ne'er be broken,
   Formed thee for his own abode:
On the Rock of Ages founded,
   What can shake thy sure repose?
With salvation's walls surrounded,
   Thou may'st smile at all thy foes.

2 See! the streams of living waters,
   Springing from eternal love,
Well supply thy sons and daughters,
   And all fear of want remove;
Who can faint while such a river
   Ever flows their thirst t' assuage?
Grace which, like the Lord, the giver,
   Never fails from age to age.

3 Round each habitation hov'ring,
   See the cloud and fire appear,
For a glory and a cov'ring —
   Showing that the Lord is near:
Glorious things of thee are spoken,
   Zion, city of our God;
He, whose word can ne'er be broken,
   Chose thee for his own abode.

WOODSTOCK. C. M.

DUTTON.

296 (1001) C. M.

BROWN.

Evening.

I LOVE to steal awhile away
  From every cumb'ring care;
And spend the hours of setting day,
  In humble, grateful prayer.

2 I love in solitude to shed
  The penitential tear;
And all his promises to plead,
  Where none but God can hear.

3 I love to think on mercies past,
  And future good implore;
And all my cares and sorrows cast
  On him whom I adore.

4 I love by faith to take a view
  Of brighter scenes in heaven:
The prospect does my strength renew,
  While here by tempests driven.

5 Thus, when life's toilsome day is o'er,
  May its departing ray
Be calm as this impressive hour,
  And lead to endless day.

297 (636) C. M.

MOORE.

Solace in Woe.

O THOU who driest the mourner's tear,
  How dark this world would be,
If, when deceived and wounded here,
  We could not fly to thee!

2 The friends who in our sunshine live,
  When winter comes are flown;
And he who has but tears to give,
  Must weep those tears alone.

3 But thou wilt heal that broken heart,
  Which, like the plants that throw
Their fragrance from the wounded part,
  Breathes sweetness out of woe.

4 When joy no longer soothes or cheers,
  And e'en the hope that threw
A moment's sparkle o'er our tears,
  Is dimmed and vanished too,—

5 O, who could bear life's stormy doom,
  Did not thy wing of love
Come brightly wafting through the gloom
  Our peace-branch from above!

LANESBORO. C. M.

298 (637) C. M.
Hope in Trouble.

WHEN musing sorrow weeps the past,
  And mourns the present pain,
'T is sweet to think of peace at last,
  And feel that death is gain.

2 'T is not that murm'ring thoughts arise,
  And dread a Father's will;
'T is not that meek submission flies,
  And would not suffer still : —

3 It is that heaven-born faith surveys
  The path that leads to light,
And longs her eagle plumes to raise,
  And lose herself in sight.—

4 It is that hope with ardor glows,
  To see him face to face,
Whose dying love no language knows
  Sufficient art to trace.

5 O let me wing my hallowed flight
  From earth-born woe and care,
And soar above these clouds of night,
  My Saviour's bliss to share !
    10 *

299 (559) C. M.   WATTS.
The Pilgrimage.

LORD ! what a wretched land is this,
  That yields us no supply,—
No cheering fruits, no wholesome trees,
  Nor streams of living joy !

2 Our journey is a thorny maze,
  But we march upward still;
Forget these troubles of the ways,
  And reach at Zion's hill.

3 See the kind angels, at the gates,
  Inviting us to come;
There Jesus, the Forerunner, waits
  To welcome trav'lers home.

4 There, on a green and flowery mount,
  Our weary souls shall sit,
And, with transporting joys, recount
  The labors of our feet.

5 No vain discourse shall fill our tongue,
  Nor trifles vex our ear ;
Infinite grace shall be our song,
  And God rejoice to hear.

H

300 (653) L. M.
Submission.

WAIT, O my soul, thy Maker's will!
  Tumultuous passions, all be still!
Nor let a murmuring thought arise;
His ways are just, his counsels wise.

2 He in the thickest darkness dwells,
Performs his work, the cause conceals;
But though his methods are unknown,
Judgment and truth support his throne.

3 Wait, then, my soul, submissive wait,
Prostrate before his awful seat:
And, midst the terrors of his rod,
Trust in a wise and gracious God.

301(1034) L. M.   C. WESLEY.
Submission to the Will of God.

ETERNAL Beam of Light divine,
  Fountain of unexhausted love;
In whom the Father's glories shine,
Through earth beneath, and heaven
    above:

2 Jesus, the weary wand'rer's rest,
Give me thy easy yoke to bear:
With steadfast patience arm my breast,
With spotless love and lowly fear.

3 Thankful I take the cup from thee,
Prepared and mingled by thy skill:
Though bitter to the taste it be,
Powerful the wounded soul to heal.

4 Be thou, O Rock of ages, nigh!
So shall each murm'ring thought be
    gone:
And grief, and fear, and care, shall fly
As clouds before the mid-day sun.

5 Speak to my warring passions, "Peace;"
Say to my trembling heart, "Be still;"
Thy power my strength and fortress is,
For all things serve thy sovereign will.

302 (688) C. M.   WATTS.
The Saints Above.

GIVE me the wings of faith, to rise
  Within the veil, and see
The saints above, how great their joys,
How bright their glories be.

2 I ask them whence their vict'ry came:
They, with united breath,
Ascribe their conquest to the Lamb,
Their triumph to his death.

3 They marked the footsteps that he trod,
His zeal inspired their breast, —
And, following their incarnate God,
Possess the promised rest.

4 Our glorious Leader claims our praise
For his own pattern given;
While the long cloud of witnesses
Show the same path to heaven.

303 (685) S. M.   C. WESLEY.
2 Cor. v. 1-9.

WE know, by faith we know,
  If this vile house of clay,
This tabernacle, sink below,
  In ruinous decay,
We have a house above,
  Not made with mortal hands;
And firm as our Redeemer's love
  That heavenly fabric stands.

2 It stands securely high,
  Indissolubly sure;
Our glorious mansion in the sky
  Shall evermore endure:
O, were we entered there!
  To perfect heaven restored!
O, were we all caught up to share
  The triumph of our Lord!

3 For this in faith we call:
  For this we weep and pray:
O, might the tabernacle fall!
  O, might we 'scape away!
Full of immortal hope,
  We urge the restless strife,
And hasten to be swallowed up
  Of everlasting life.

FREDERICK. 11s. KINGSLEY.

304 **(708)** 11s. MUHLENBERG.
"I would not live alway."

I WOULD not live alway: I ask not
to stay [the way;
Where storm after storm rises dark o'er
The few lurid mornings that dawn on us
here [for its cheer.
Are enough for life's woes, full enough

2 I would not live alway: no — welcome
the tomb, [its gloom;
Since Jesus hath lain there, I dread not
There sweet be my rest, till he bid me
arise, [skies.
To hail him in triumph descending the

3 Who, who would live alway, away from
his God,— [abode,
Away from yon heaven, that blissful
Where the rivers of pleasure flow o'er
the bright plains, [reigns:
And the noontide of glory eternally

4 Where the saints of all ages in harmony
meet, [to greet;
Their Saviour and brethren, transported

While the anthems of rapture unceas-
ingly roll, [of the soul !
And the smile of the Lord is the feast

305 **(487)** 11s.
Heaven below.

MY God, I am thine, What a comfort
divine, [is mine !
What a blessing to know that my Jesus
In the heavenly Lamb, Thrice happy I
am, — [his name.
My heart doth rejoice at the sound of

2 True pleasures abound In the rapturous
sound, [found:
Whoever hath found it, hath paradise
My Jesus to know, And feel his blood
flow, —
'T is life everlasting, 't is heaven below.

3 Yet onward I haste To the heavenly
feast: [taste !
That, that is the fulness; but this is the
And this I shall prove, Till with joy I
remove
To the heaven of heavens in Jesus' love.

306 (668) C. M.

Psalm xc.

O GOD, our help in ages past,
   Our hope for years to come,
Our shelter from the stormy blast,
   And our eternal home:

2 Under the shadow of thy throne,
   Still may we dwell secure ;
Sufficient is thine arm alone,
   And our defence is sure.

3 Before the hills in order stood,
   Or earth received her frame,
From everlasting thou art God,
   To endless years the same.

4 A thousand ages, in thy sight,
   Are like an evening gone ;
Short as the watch that ends the night
   Before the rising sun.

5 The busy tribes of flesh and blood,
   With all their cares and fears,
Are carried downward by the flood,
   And lost in following years.

6 Time, like an ever-rolling stream,
   Bears all its sons away ;
They fly, forgotten, as a dream
   Dies at the op'ning day.

7 O God, our help in ages past,
   Our hope for years to come ;
Be thou our guard while life shall last,
   And our perpetual home!

307 (674) S. M.   C. WESLEY.

The End of Life.

AND am I born to die?
   To lay this body down?
And must my trembling spirit fly
   Into a world unknown ? —
A land of deepest shade,
   Unpierced by human thought;
The dreary regions of the dead,
   Where all things are forgot!

2 Soon as from earth I go,
   What will become of me?
Eternal happiness or woe
   Must then my portion be !
Waked by the trumpet's sound,
   I from my grave shall rise;
And see the Judge with glory crowned,
   And see the flaming skies !

3 How shall I leave my tomb —
   With triumph or regret?
A fearful or a joyful doom,
   A curse or blessing meet?
Will angel bands convey
   Their brother to the bar?
Or devils drag my soul away
   To meet its sentence there ?

4 Who can resolve the doubt
   That tears my anxious breast?
Shall I be with the damned cast out,
   Or numbered with the blest?
I must from God be driven,
   Or with my Saviour dwell ;
Must come at his command to heaven,
   Or else — depart to hell.

308 (715) C. M.   C. WESLEY.

The Full Assurance of Hope.

O WHAT a blessed hope is ours!
   While here on earth we stay,
We more than taste the heavenly powers,
   And antedate that day :
We feel the resurrection near,
   Our life in Christ concealed,
And with his glorious presence here
   Our earthen vessels filled.

2 O, would he more of heaven bestow,
   And let the vessels break,
And let our ransomed spirits go,
   To grasp the God we seek ;
In rapt'rous awe on him to gaze,
   Who bought the sight for me,
And shout, and wonder at his grace
   To all eternity !

309 (705) C. M.
The Heavenly Jerusalem.

JERUSALEM, my happy home!
  Name ever dear to me!
When shall my labors have an end,
  In joy, and peace, and thee?

2 When shall these eyes thy heaven-built
    walls
And pearly gates behold?
Thy bulwarks, with salvation strong,
  And streets of shining gold?

3 O when, thou city of my God,
  Shall I thy courts ascend,
Where congregations ne'er break up,
  And Sabbaths have no end?

4 There happier bowers than Eden's bloom,
  Nor sin nor sorrow know:
Blest seats! through rude and stormy
    scenes
I onward press to you.

5 Why should I shrink at pain and woe?
  Or feel at death dismay?
I 've Canaan's goodly land in view,
  And realms of endless day.

6 Apostles, martyrs, prophets, there,
  Around my Saviour stand;
And soon my friends in Christ below
  Will join the glorious band.

7 Jerusalem! my happy home!
  My soul still pants for thee;
Then shall my labors have an end,
  When I thy joys shall see.

310 (706) C. M.   WATTS.
The Heavenly Canaan.

THERE is a land of pure delight,
  Where saints immortal reign;
Infinite day excludes the night,
  And pleasures banish pain.

2 There everlasting spring abides,
  And never-with'ring flowers:
Death, like a narrow sea, divides
  This heavenly land from ours.

3 Sweet fields beyond the swelling flood
  Stand dressed in living green;
So to the Jews old Canaan stood,
  While Jordan rolled between.

4 Could we but climb where Moses stood,
  And view the landscape o'er,
Not Jordan's stream, nor death's cold
    flood,
Should fright us from the shore.

311 (707) C. M.   S. STENNETT.
The Heavenly Canaan.

ON Jordan's stormy banks I stand,
  And cast a wishful eye
To Canaan's fair and happy land,
  Where my possessions lie.

2 O, the transporting, rapt'rous scene
  That rises to my sight!
Sweet fields arrayed in living green,
  And rivers of delight!

3 There gen'rous fruits that never fail
  On trees immortal grow:
There rocks, and hills, and brooks, and
    vales,
With milk and honey flow.

4 All o'er those wide-extended plains
  Shines one eternal day;
There God, the Sun, for ever reigns,
  And scatters night away.

5 No chilling winds nor pois'nous breath
  Can reach that healthful shore;
Sickness and sorrow, pain and death,
  Are felt and feared no more.

6 When shall I reach that happy place,
  And be for ever blest?
When shall I see my Father's face,
  And in his bosom rest?

7 Filled with delight, my raptured soul
  Would here no longer stay!
Though Jordan's waves around me roll,
  Fearless I 'd launch away.

TYRONE. C. M.

312 (712) C. M.   C. WESLEY.

Visions of Heaven.

O WHAT hath Jesus bought for me!
　　Before my ravished eyes
Rivers of life divine I see,
　　And trees of paradise!

2 They flourish in perpetual bloom,
　　Fruit every month they give;
And to the healing leaves who come,
　　Eternally shall live.

3 I see a world of spirits bright,
　　Who reap the pleasures there!
They all are robed in spotless white,
　　And conq'ring palms they bear:

4 Adorned by their Redeemer's grace,
　　They close pursue the Lamb,
And every shining front displays
　　Th' unutterable name.

5 O, what are all my suff'rings here,
　　If, Lord, thou count me meet
With that enraptured host t' appear,
　　And worship at thy feet!

6 Give joy or grief, give ease or pain: —
　　Take life or friends away,
I come to find them all again
　　In that eternal day.

313 (716) C. M.   C. WESLEY.

The Whole Family in Heaven and Earth.

COME, let us join our friends above,
　　That have obtained the prize;
And on the eagle wings of love
　　To joys celestial rise:

2 Let all the saints terrestrial sing,
　　With those to glory gone;
For all the servants of our King,
　　In earth and heaven, are one.

3 One family we dwell in him,
　　One Church above, beneath,
Though now divided by the stream,
　　The narrow stream of death.

4 One army of the living God,
　　To his command we bow;
Part of his host have crossed the flood,
　　And part are crossing now.

5 Ten thousand to their endless home
　　This solemn moment fly;
And we are to the margin come,
　　And we expect to die:

6 His militant embodied host,
　　With wishful looks we stand,
And long to see that happy coast,
　　And reach the heavenly land.

BRATTLE STREET. C. M. PLEYEL.

314 (713) C. M. C. WESLEY.
The Full Assurance of Hope.

HOW happy every child of grace,
 Who knows his sins forgiven!
This earth, he cries, is not my place,
 I seek my place in heaven;
A country far from mortal sight: —
 Yet, O! by faith I see
The land of rest, the saints' delight,
 The heaven prepared for me.

2 A stranger in the world below,
 I calmly sojourn here;
Nor can its happiness or woe
 Provoke my hope or fear;
Its evils in a moment end,
 Its joys as soon are past!
But O! the bliss to which I tend
 Eternally shall last.

3 To that Jerusalem above
 With singing I repair;
While in the flesh, my hope and love,
 My heart and soul are there.
There my exalted Saviour stands
 My merciful High Priest,
And still extends his wounded hands,
 To take me to his breast.

315 (711) C. M. C. WESLEY.
Visions of Heaven.

AND let this feeble body fail,
 And let it droop or die:
My soul shall quit the mournful vale,
 And soar to worlds on high,—
Shall join the disembodied saints,
 And find its long-sought rest,
That only bliss for which it pants,
 In my Redeemer's breast.

2 In hope of that immortal crown,
 I now the cross sustain;
And gladly wander up and down,
 And smile at toil and pain:
I suffer out my threescore years,
 Till my Deliv'rer come,
And wipe away his servant's tears,
 And take his exile home.

3 Surely he will not long delay:
 I hear his Spirit cry,
"Arise, my love, make haste away!
 Go, get thee up and die.
O'er death, who now has lost his sting,
 I give thee victory;
And with me my reward I bring,
 I bring my heaven for thee."

I. BAPTISM.

316 (531) S. M.   C. WESLEY.

The Act of Consecration.

LORD, in the strength of grace,
  With a glad heart and free,
Myself, my residue of days,
  I consecrate to thee.

2 Thy ransomed servant, I   .
  Restore to thee thy own;
And, from this moment, live or die
  To serve my God alone.

317 (285) C. M.   DODDRIDGE.

Infant. — Mark x. 13-16.

SEE Israel's gentle Shepherd stand
  With all-engaging charms:
Hark how he calls the tender lambs,
  And folds them in his arms!

2 "Permit them to approach," he cries,
  "Nor scorn their humble name:
For 't was to bless such souls as these
  The Lord of angels came."

3 We bring them, Lord, in thankful hands,
  And yield them up to thee;
Joyful that we ourselves are thine,
  Thine let our offspring be.

318 (286) C. M.   WATTS.

Infant.

THUS Lydia sanctified her house,
  When she received the word;
Thus the believing jailer gave
  His household to the Lord.

2 Thus later saints, eternal King,
  Thine ancient truth embrace:
To thee their infant offspring bring,
  And humbly claim the grace.

319 (279) L. M.   WATTS.

The Commission. — For Adults.

'TWAS the commission of our Lord,
  "Go, teach the nations, and bap-
      tize:"
The nations have received the word
  Since he ascended to the skies.

2 "Repent, and be baptized," he saith,
  "For the remission of your sins;"
And thus our sense assists our faith,
  And shows us what his gospel means.

3 Our souls he washes in his blood,
  As water makes the body clean;
And the good Spirit from our God
  Descends like purifying rain.

4 Thus we engage ourselves to thee,
  And seal our covenant with the Lord:
O may the great Eternal Three
  In heaven our solemn vows record!

320 (281) S. M.   W. M. BUNTING.

Adult.

RITES change not, Lord, the heart,—
  Undo the evil done,—
Or, with the uttered name, impart
  The nature of thy Son.

2 To meet our desp'rate want,
  There gushed a mystic flood;
O from his heart's o'erflowing font
  Baptize this soul with blood!

3 Be grace from Christ our Lord,
  And love from God supreme,
By the communing Spirit poured
  In a perpetual stream.

321 (282) 6s & 8s.   C. WESLEY.

Adult.

BAPTIZED into thy name,
  Mysterious One in Three,
Our souls and bodies claim
  A sacrifice to thee:
We only live our faith to prove,
The faith which works by humble love.

II. THE LORD'S SUPPER.

322 (294) L. M.

The Table Prepared.

* * * * * * * *

HAIL, sacred feast, which Jesus
  makes!
Rich banquet of his flesh and blood!
Thrice happy he who here partakes
That sacred stream, that heavenly
  food!

3 Why are its bounties all in vain
Before unwilling hearts displayed?
Was not for you the Victim slain?
Are you forbid the children's bread?

4 O let thy table honored be,
And furnished well with joyful guests!
And may each soul salvation see,
That here its sacred pledges tastes!

5 Let crowds approach with hearts pre-
  pared;
With hearts inflamed let all attend;
Nor, when we leave our Father's board,
The pleasure or the profit end.

323 (290) C. M.   NOEL.

" This do in remembrance of me."

IF human kindness meets return,
  And owns the grateful tie;
If tender thoughts within us burn
To feel a friend is nigh; —

2 O shall not warmer accents tell
The gratitude we owe
To him who died our fears to quell,
Our more than orphan's woe!

3 While yet his anguished soul surveyed
Those pangs he would not flee;
What love his latest words displayed, —
" Meet and remember me! "

4 Remember thee! thy death, thy shame,
Our sinful hearts to share!
O mem'ry, leave no other name
But his recorded there!

11

324 (291) C. M.   MONTGOMERY.

Remembering Christ.

ACCORDING to thy gracious word,
  In meek humility,
This will I do, my dying Lord,
I will remember thee.

2 Thy body, broken for my sake,
My bread from heaven shall be;
Thy testamental cup I take,
And thus remember thee.

3 Gethsemane can I forget?
Or there thy conflict see,
Thine agony and bloody sweat,
And not remember thee?

4 When to the cross I turn mine eyes,
And rest on Calvary,
O Lamb of God, my Sacrifice,
I must remember thee!

5 Remember thee and all thy pains,
And all thy love to me;
Yea, while a breath, a pulse remains,
Will I remember thee.

325 (304) 8s & 7s.   C. WESLEY.

" It is the Spirit that quickeneth."

COME, thou everlasting Spirit,
  Bring to every thankful mind
All the Saviour's dying merit,
  All his suff'rings for mankind:
True recorder of his passion,
  Now the living faith impart,
Now reveal his great salvation,
  Preach his gospel to our heart.

2 Come, thou witness of his dying,
  Come, remembrancer divine,
Let us feel thy power applying
  Christ to every soul and mine:
Let us groan thine inward groaning,
  Look on Him we pierced and grieve,
All receive the grace atoning,
  All the sprinkled blood receive.

MARLOW. C. M.

Moderato.

326 (295) C. M.   DODDRIDGE.
The Invitation.

THE King of heaven his table spreads,
And blessings crown the board:
Not paradise, with all its joys,
Could such delight afford.

2 Pardon and peace to dying men,
And endless life, are given;
Through the rich blood that Jesus shed
To raise our souls to heaven.

3 Millions of souls, in glory now,
Were fed and feasted here;
And millions more, still on the way,
Around the board appear.

4 All things are ready; come away,
Nor weak excuses frame;
Crowd to your places at the feast,
And bless the Founder's name.

327 (288) C. M.   HART.
The Institution.

THAT doleful night before his death,
The Lamb for sinners slain
Did, almost with his dying breath,
This solemn feast ordain.

2 To keep the feast, Lord, we have met,
And to remember thee:
Help each poor trembler to repeat,
"For me, he died for me!"

3 Thy suff'rings, Lord, each sacred sign
To our remembrance brings;
We eat the bread, and drink the wine,
But think on nobler things.

4 O tune our tongues, and set in frame
Each heart that pants for thee,
To sing, "Hosanna to the Lamb!"
The Lamb that died for me!

328 (292) C. M.   WATTS.
The Covenant Sealed.

THE promise of my Father's love
Shall stand for ever good:
He said, and gave his soul to death,
And sealed the grace with blood.

2 To this dear cov'nant of thy word
I set my worthless name;
I seal th' engagement to my Lord,
And make my humble claim.

3 Thy light, and strength, and pard'ning
grace,
And glory, shall be mine;
My life and soul, my heart and flesh,
And all my powers, are thine.

LISBON. S. M.

III. THE SABBATH.

329 (313) S. M. WATTS.

Opening Morning Service.

WELCOME, sweet day of rest,
  That saw the Lord arise:
Welcome to this reviving breast,
And these rejoicing eyes!

2 The King himself comes near,
  And feasts his saints to-day:
Here we may sit, and see him here,
And love, and praise, and pray.

3 One day within the place
  Which thou dost, Lord, frequent,
Is sweeter than ten thousand days
In sinful pleasures spent.

4 My willing soul would stay
  In such a frame as this,
And sit and sing herself away
To everlasting bliss.

330 (217) S. M. C. WESLEY.

Work and Witness.

O COME, and dwell in me,
  Spirit of power within!
And bring the glorious liberty
From sorrow, fear, and sin.

2 This inward, dire disease,
  Spirit of health, remove,
Spirit of finished holiness,
Spirit of perfect love.

3 Hasten the joyful day
  Which shall my sins consume,
When old things shall be done away,
And all things new become.

4 I want the witness, Lord,
  That all I do is right,
According to thy will and word,
Well pleasing in thy sight.

5 I ask no higher state;
  Indulge me but in this;
And soon or later then translate
To my eternal bliss.

331 (271) S. M. C. WESLEY.

For an Increase of Laborers.

LORD of the harvest, hear
  Thy needy servants' cry;
Answer our faith's effectual prayer,
And all our wants supply.

2 On thee we humbly wait,
  Our wants are in thy view;
The harvest truly, Lord, is great,
The laborers are few.

3 Convert, and send forth more
  Into thy Church abroad,
And let them speak thy word of power,
As workers with their God.

4 O let them spread thy name,
  Their mission fully prove;
Thy universal grace proclaim,
Thine all-redeeming love!

332 (314) C. M.   C. WESLEY.

Opening Morning Service.

COME, let us join with one accord
  In hymns around the throne!
This is the day our rising Lord
  Hath made and called his own.

2 This is the day which God hath blest,
  The brightest of the seven,
Type of that everlasting rest
  The saints enjoy in heaven.

3 Then let us in his name sing on,
  And hasten to that day
When our Redeemer shall come down,
  And shadows pass away.

333 (1009) C. M.   WILLIAMS.

" My meditation of him shall be sweet."

WHILE thee I seek, protecting
    Power!
Be my vain wishes stilled;
And may this consecrated hour
With better hopes be filled.

2 Thy love the power of thought bestowed,
  To thee my thoughts would soar:
Thy mercy o'er my life has flowed,
  That mercy I adore.

3 In each event of life, how clear
  Thy ruling hand I see!
Each blessing to my soul most dear,
  Because conferred by thee.

4 In every joy that crowns my days,
  In every pain I bear,
My heart shall find delight in praise,
  Or seek relief in prayer.

5 When gladness wings the favored hour,
  Thy love my thoughts shall fill;
Resigned, when storms of sorrow lower,
  My soul shall meet thy will.

6 My lifted eye, without a tear,
  The gath'ring storm shall see;
My steadfast heart shall know no fear—
  That heart will rest on thee.

334 (316) L. M.   STENNETT.

Opening Morning Service.

ANOTHER six days' work is done;
  Another Sabbath is begun:
Return, my soul, enjoy thy rest,
Improve the day thy God hath blest.

2 O that our thoughts and thanks may rise,
As grateful incense to the skies;
And draw from Christ that sweet repose
Which none but he that feels it knows!

3 This heavenly calm within the breast
Is the dear pledge of glorious rest
Which for the Church of God remains,
The end of cares, the end of pains.

4 In holy duties let the day,
In holy comforts pass away:
How sweet, a Sabbath thus to spend,
In hope of one that ne'er shall end!

335 (1002) L. M.   EDMESTON.

A Sabbath Evening Meditation.

IS there a time when moments flow
  More lovelily than all beside?
It is, of all the times below,
  A Sabbath eve in summer tide.

2 O then the setting sun smiles fair,
  And all below, and all above,
The diff'rent forms of nature wear
  One universal garb of love.

3 And then the peace that Jesus beams,
  The life of grace, the death of sin,
With nature's placid woods and streams,
  Is peace without, and peace within.

4 Delightful scene!—a world at rest—
  A God all love—no grief nor fear—
A heavenly hope—a peaceful breast—
  A smile unsullied by a tear!

5 Yet will there dawn at last a day,
  A sun that never sets shall rise;
Night will not veil his ceaseless ray;
  The heavenly Sabbath never dies!

ORFORD. L. M.

L. MASON.

336 **(320)** L. M. WATTS.

Psalm xcii.

SWEET is the work, my God, my King,
To praise thy name, give thanks, and
sing;
To show thy love by morning light,
And talk of all thy truth by night.

2 Sweet is the day of sacred rest;
No mortal cares shall seize my breast:
O may my heart in tune be found,
Like David's harp of solemn sound!

3 My heart shall triumph in my Lord,
And bless his works, and bless his word:
Thy works of grace, how bright they
shine!
How deep thy counsels! how divine!

4 Then I shall share a glorious part
When grace hath well refined my heart,
And fresh supplies of joy are shed,
Like holy oil, to cheer my head.

5 Then shall I see, and hear, and know,
All I desired or wished below;
And every power find sweet employ
In that eternal world of joy.

11 *

337 **(324)** L. M. DODDRIDGE.

The Eternal Sabbath.

THINE earthly Sabbaths, Lord, we
love;
But there's a nobler rest above;
To that our lab'ring souls aspire,
With ardent pangs of strong desire.

2 No more fatigue, no more distress;
Nor sin nor hell shall reach the place;
No sighs shall mingle with the songs
Which warble from immortal tongues.

3 No rude alarms of raging foes;
No cares to break the long repose;
No midnight shade, no clouded sun,
But sacred, high, eternal noon.

4 O long-expected day, begin;
Dawn on these realms of woe and sin:
Fain would we leave this weary road,
And sleep in death, to rest with God.

Doxology.

Praise God, from whom all blessings flow;
Praise him, all creatures here below;
Praise him above, ye heavenly host;
Praise Father, Son, and Holy Ghost.

DEDHAM. C. M.

IV. BURIAL OF THE DEAD.

338 (667) C. M.   WATTS.

Psalm xxxix.

TEACH me the measure of my days,
   Thou Maker of my frame:
I would survey life's narrow space,
And learn how frail I am.

2 A span is all that we can boast,
   An inch or two of time:
Man is but vanity and dust,
   In all his flower and prime.

3 What should I wish, or wait for, then,
   From creatures, earth, and dust?
They make our expectations vain,
   And disappoint our trust.

4 Now I forbid my carnal hope,
   My fond desires recall;
I give my mortal interest up,
   And make my God my all.

339 (669) C. M.   WATTS.

Brevity of Life.

THEE we adore, eternal Name!
   And humbly own to thee
How feeble is our mortal frame,
What dying worms we be!

2 The year rolls round, and steals away
   The breath that first it gave:
Whate'er we do, where'er we be,
   We 're travelling to the grave.

3 Dangers stand thick through all the
      ground,
To push us to the tomb;
And fierce diseases wait around
   To hurry mortals home.

4 Great God! on what a slender thread
   Hang everlasting things!
Th' eternal states of all the dead
   Upon life's feeble strings.

5 Infinite joy, or endless woe,
   Attends on every breath;
And yet how unconcerned we go
   Upon the brink of death!

6 Waken, O Lord, our drowsy sense,
   To walk this dangerous road;
And if our souls be hurried hence,
   May they be found with God!

Doxology.

Now let the Father, and the Son,
   And Spirit be adored,
Where there are works to make him
      [known,
Or saints to love the Lord.

340 (679) L. M.   WATTS.
The Peaceful Death.

WHY should we start and fear to die;
  What tim'rous worms we mortals
      are!
Death is the gate to endless joy,
And yet we dread to enter there.

2 The pains, the groans, the dying strife,
  Fright our approaching souls away;
And we shrink back again to life,
  Fond of our prison and our clay.

3 O, if my Lord would come and meet,
  My soul would stretch her wings in
      haste,
Fly fearless through death's iron gate,
  Nor feel the terrors as she passed!

4 Jesus can make a dying bed
  Feel soft as downy pillows are,
While on his breast I lean my head,
  And breathe my life out sweetly there.

341 (723) C. M.   STEELE.
Funeral of a Young Person.

WHEN blooming youth is snatched
  away
By death's resistless hand,
Our hearts the mournful tribute pay,
  Which pity must demand.

2 While pity prompts the rising sigh,
  O may this truth, impressed
With awful power — I too must die —
  Sink deep in every breast!

3 Let this vain world delude no more:
  Behold the gaping tomb!
It bids us seize the present hour,
  To-morrow death may come.

4 The voice of this alarming scene
  Let every heart obey;
Nor be the heavenly warning vain,
  Which calls to watch and pray.

342 (1046) 8s & 7s. C. WESLEY.
To the Departing Saint.

HAPPY soul, thy days are ended,
  All thy mourning days below;
Go, by angel guards attended,
  To the sight of Jesus, go!

Waiting to receive thy spirit,
  Lo! the Saviour stands above, —
Shows the purchase of his merit,
  Reaches out the crown of love. ◆

2 Struggle through thy latest passion,
  To thy great Redeemer's breast,
To his uttermost salvation,
  To his everlasting rest.
For the joy he sets before thee,
  Bear a momentary pain —
Die, to live a life of glory!
  Suffer, with thy Lord to reign.

343 (681) L. M.   BARBAULD.
Death of the Righteous.

HOW blest the righteous when he dies!
  When sinks a weary soul to rest,
How mildly beam the closing eyes!
  How gently heaves th' expiring breast!

2 So fades a summer cloud away:
  So sinks the gale when storms are o'er;
So gently shuts the eye of day;
  So dies a wave along the shore.

3 Life's duty done, as sinks the clay,
  Light from its load the spirit flies:
While heaven and earth combine to say,
  "How blest the righteous when he
     dies!"

344 (721) C. M.   STEELE.
Funeral of a Child.

LIFE is a span, a fleeting hour, —
  How soon the vapor flies!
Man is a tender, transient flower,
  That e'en in blooming dies.

2 Death spreads his with'ring, wintry arms,
  And beauty smiles no more:
Ah! where are now those rising charms
  Which pleased our eyes before?

3 That once loved form, now cold and
     dead,
  Each mournful thought employs;
We weep our earthly comforts fled,
  And withered all our joys.

4 Hope looks beyond the bounds of time,
  When what we now deplore,
Shall rise in full, immortal prime,
  And bloom to fade no more.

ASHVILLE. C. M.

Slow.

345 (670) C. M.   Heber.

Dwelling among the Tombs.

BENEATH our feet and o'er our head
   Is equal warning given:
Beneath us lie the countless dead,
   Above us is the heaven!

2 Their names are graven on the stone,
   Their bones are in the clay;
And ere another day is gone
   Ourselves may be as they.

3 Death rides on every passing breeze,
   And lurks in every flower;
Each season has its own disease,
   Its peril every hour!

4 Our eyes have seen the rosy light
   Of youth's soft cheek decay,
And fate descend in sudden night
   On manhood's middle day.

5 Our eyes have seen the steps of age
   Halt feebly to the tomb;
And yet shall earth our hearts engage,
   And dreams of days to come?

6 Turn, mortal, turn! thy danger know:
   Where'er thy foot can tread,
The earth rings hollow from below,
   And warns thee of her dead!

7 Turn, Christian, turn! thy soul apply
   To truths divinely given:
The forms which underneath thee lie
   Shall live for hell or heaven!

346 (671) C. M.   Watts.

A Voice from the Tombs.

HARK! from the tombs a doleful
   sound!
My ears, attend the cry:
" Ye living men, come view the ground
   Where you must shortly lie.

2 " Princes, this clay must be your bed,
   In spite of all your towers;
The tall, the wise, the reverend head,
   Must lie as low as ours."

3 Great God! is this our certain doom!
   And are we still secure!
Still walking downward to the tomb,
   And yet prepared no more!

4 Grant us the power of quick'ning grace,
   To fit our souls to fly;
Then, when we drop this dying flesh,
   We 'll rise above the sky.

ONIDO. 7s.

347 (702) 7s.　　C. WESLEY.
Rev. vii. 13-17.

WHAT are these arrayed in white,
　Brighter than the noonday sun;
Foremost of the sons of light,
　Nearest the eternal throne?
These are they that bore the cross,
　Nobly for their Master stood;
Suff'rers in his righteous cause,
　Foll'wers of the dying God.

2 Out of great distress they came,
　Washed their robes by faith below
In the blood of yonder Lamb,
　Blood that washes white as snow;
Therefore are they next the throne,
　Serve their Maker day and night:
God resides among his own,
　God doth in his saints delight.

348 (1045) 7s.　　TOPLADY.
The dying Christian to his Soul.

DEATHLESS principle, arise;
　Soar, thou native of the skies.
Pearl of price by Jesus bought,
To his glorious likeness wrought,
Go to shine before his throne,
Deck his mediatorial crown:
Go, his triumphs to adorn;
Made for God, to God return.

2 Lo! he beckons from on high;
Fearless to his presence fly:
Thine the merit of his blood;
Thine the righteousness of God.
Angels, joyful to attend,
Hov'ring round thy pillow bend,
Wait to catch the signal given,
And escort thee quick to heaven.

I

SAUL. L. M.

HANDEL.

349 (724) L. M.   S. WESLEY, JR.

Funeral of a Youth.—1 *Peter* i. 24, 25.

THE morning flowers display their
    sweets,
    And gay their silken leaves unfold,
As careless of the noontide heats,
    As fearless of the evening cold.

2 Nipped by the wind's untimely blast,
    Parched by the sun's directer ray,
The momentary glories waste,
    The short-lived beauties die away.

3 So blooms the human face divine,
    When youth its pride of beauty shows:
Fairer than spring the colors shine,
    And sweeter than the virgin rose.

4 Or worn by slowly rolling years,
    Or broke by sickness in a day,
The fading glory disappears,
    The short-lived beauties die away.

350 (728) L. M.   WATTS.

Funeral of a Christian.

UNVEIL thy bosom, faithful tomb,
    Take this new treasure to thy trust:
And give these sacred relics room,
    To slumber in the silent dust.

2 Nor pain, nor grief, nor anxious fear,
    Invades thy bounds; no mortal woes
Can reach the peaceful sleeper here,
    While angels watch the soft repose.

3 So Jesus slept: God's dying Son
    Passed through the grave, and blessed
       the bed:
Rest here, blest saint, till from his throne
    The morning break, and pierce the
       shade.

4 Break from his throne, illustrious morn!
    Attend, O earth, his sovereign word!
Restore thy trust: a glorious form
    Shall then arise to meet the Lord.

PLEYEL'S HYMN. 7s.

351 (727) 7s. C. WESLEY.

Funeral of a Christian. — Rev. xiv. 13.

HARK! a voice divides the sky,
Happy are the faithful dead!
In the Lord who sweetly die,
They from all their toils are freed.

2 Them the Spirit hath declared
Blest, unutterably blest:
Jesus is their great reward,
Jesus is their endless rest.

3 Followed by their works, they go
Where their Head has gone before:
Reconciled by grace below,
Grace hath opened Mercy's door.

4 Justified through faith alone,
Here they knew their sins forgiven;
Here they laid their burden down,
Hallowed, and made meet for heaven.

352 (733) 7s. C. WESLEY.

Funeral of a Christian Sister.

LO! the pris'ner is released,
Lightened of her fleshly load:

Where the weary are at rest,
She is gathered into God!
Lo! the pain of life is past,
All her warfare now is o'er;
Death and hell behind are cast,
Grief and suffering are no more.

2 Yes, the Christian's course is run,
Ended is the glorious strife;
Fought the fight, the work is done,
Death is swallowed up of life!
Borne by angels on their wings,
Far from earth the spirit flies,
Finds her God, and sits, and sings,
Triumphing in paradise.

3 Let the world bewail their dead,
Fondly of their loss complain:
Sister! friend! by Jesus freed,
Death, to thee, to us, is gain:
Thou art entered into joy;
Let the unbelievers mourn;
We in songs our lives employ
Till we all to God return.

Dozology.

Sing we to our God above,
Praise eternal as his love;
Praise him, all ye heavenly host —
Father, Son, and Holy Ghost.

CHINA. C. M.

353 (729) C. M.   WATTS.

Funeral of a Christian.

WHY do we mourn departing friends,
  Or shake at death's alarms?
'T is but the voice that Jesus sends,
  To call them to his arms.

2 Are we not tending upward too,
  As fast as time can move?
Nor should we wish the hours more slow
  To keep us from our Love.

3 Why should we tremble to convey
  Their bodies to the tomb?
There once the flesh of Jesus lay,
  And left a long perfume.

4 The graves of all his saints be blessed,
  And softened every bed:
Where should the dying members rest,
  But with their dying Head?

5 Thence he arose, ascending high
  And showed our feet the way:
Up to the Lord our flesh shall fly,
  At the great rising day.

6 Then let the last loud trumpet sound,
  And bid our kindred rise:
Awake, ye nations under ground;
  Ye saints, ascend the skies!

354 (737) C. M.   DODDRIDGE.

Funeral of a Minister.

WHAT though the arm of conqu'ring
      death
Does God's own house invade?
What though the prophet and the priest
  Be numbered with the dead?

2 Though earthly shepherds dwell in dust,
  The aged and the young,—
The watchful eye in darkness closed,
  And mute th' instructive tongue,—

3 Th' Eternal Shepherd still survives,
  New comfort to impart;
His eye still guides us, and his voice
  Still animates our heart.

4 "Lo! I am with you," saith the Lord,
  "My Church shall safe abide;
For I will ne'er forsake my own,
  Whose souls in me confide."

5 Through every scene of life and death,
  This promise is our trust;
And this shall be our children's song,
  When we are cold in dust.

DUKE STREET. L. M.

V. MISSIONS.

355 (195) L. M. WATTS.

The Grace of Christ.

NOW to the Lord a noble song!
Awake, my soul; awake, my tongue:
Hosanna to th' Eternal Name,
And all his boundless love proclaim.

2 See, where it shines in Jesus' face,
The brightest image of his grace:
God, in the person of his Son,
Has all his mightiest works outdone.

3 The spacious earth and spreading flood
Proclaim the wise, the powerful God;
And thy rich glories from afar,
Sparkle in every rolling star:

4 But in his looks a glory stands,
The noblest labor of thy hands:
The pleasing lustre of his eyes
Outshines the wonders of the skies.

5 Grace!—'tis a sweet, a charming theme:
My thoughts rejoice at Jesus' name!
Ye angels, dwell upon the sound;
Ye heavens, reflect it to the ground!

6 O may I reach the happy place
Where he unveils his lovely face!
Where all his beauties you behold,
And sing his name to harps of gold.

12

356 (741) L. M. WATTS.

Psalm lxxii.

JESUS shall reign where'er the sun
Does his successive journeys run;
His kingdom stretch from shore to shore,
Till moons shall wax and wane no more.

2 From north to south the princes meet
To pay their homage at his feet;
While western empires own their Lord,
And savage tribes attend his word.

3 For him shall endless prayer be made,
And endless praises crown his head;
His name, like sweet perfume, shall rise
With every morning sacrifice.

4 People and realms, of every tongue,
Dwell on his love with sweetest song,
And infant voices shall proclaim
Their early blessings on his name.

5 Blessings abound where'er he reigns,
The pris'ner leaps to loose his chains,
The weary find eternal rest,
And all the sons of want are blessed.

6 Let every creature rise and bring
Peculiar honors to our King;
Angels descend with songs again,
And earth repeat the long Amen!

357 (757) S. M.   C. WESLEY.
God giveth the increase.

LORD, if at thy command
    The word of life we sow,
Watered by thy almighty hand,
    The seed shall surely grow:
The virtue of thy grace
    A large increase shall give,.
And multiply the faithful race,
    Who to thy glory live.

2 Now, then, the ceaseless shower
    Of gospel blessings send,
And let the soul-converting power
    Thy ministers attend.
On multitudes confer
    The heart-renewing love,
And by the joy of grace prepare
    For fuller joys above.

358 (765) 7s.   BOWRING.
"Watchman, what of the night?"

WATCHMAN, tell us of the night,
    What its signs of promise are.
Trav'ller, o'er yon mountain's height,
    See that glory-beaming star.
Watchman, does its beauteous ray
Aught of hope or joy foretell?
Trav'ller, yes; it brings the day,
    Promised day of Israel.

2 Watchman, tell us of the night;
    Higher yet that star ascends.
Trav'ller, blessedness and light,
    Peace and truth, its course portends.
Watchman, will its beams alone
Gild the spot that gave them birth?
Trav'ller, ages are its own,
    See! it bursts o'er all the earth.

3 Watchman, tell us of the night,
    For the morning seems to dawn.
Trav'ller, darkness takes its flight,
    Doubt and terror are withdrawn.
Watchman, let thy wand'rings cease;
Hie thee to thy quiet home.
Trav'ller, lo! the Prince of peace,
    Lo! the Son of God is come.

359 (225) L. M.   MONTGOMERY.
His Universal Effusion.

O SPIRIT of the living God!
    In all the fulness of thy grace,
Where'er the foot of man hath trod,
    Descend on our apostate race.

2 Give tongues of fire and hearts of love
    To preach the reconciling word:
Give power and unction from above,
    Whene'er the joyful sound is heard.

3 Be darkness, at thy coming, light;
    Confusion, order, in thy path;
Souls without strength, inspire with
        might;
    Bid mercy triumph over wrath!

4 Baptize the nations! far and nigh
    The triumphs of the cross record:
The name of Jesus glorify,
    Till every kindred call him Lord.

360 (767) 7s.   C. WESLEY.
Success.

SEE how great a flame aspires,
    Kindled by a spark of grace!
Jesus' love the nations fires,
    Sets the kingdoms on a blaze.
To bring fire on earth he came;
    Kindled in some hearts it is:
O that all might catch the flame,
    All partake the glorious bliss!

2 When he first the work begun,
    Small and feeble was his day:
Now the word doth swiftly run,
    Now it wins its widening way:
More and more it spreads and grows,
    Ever mighty to prevail;
Sin's strongholds it now o'erthrows,
    Shakes the trembling gates of hell.

3 Saw ye not the cloud arise,
    Little as a human hand?
Now it spreads along the skies,
    Hangs o'er all the thirsty land;
Lo! the promise of a shower
    Drops already from above;
But the Lord will shortly pour
    All the Spirit of his love.

WILMOT. 8s & 7s.

WEBER.

Bold.

361 (762) 8s & 7s.

" Freely ye have received — freely give."

PRAISE the Saviour, all ye nations,
 Praise him, all ye hosts above;
Shout, with joyful acclamations,
 His divine, victorious love:
Be his kingdom now promoted,
 Let the earth her monarch know;
Be my all to him devoted,
 To my Lord my all I owe.

2 See how beauteous on the mountains
 Are their feet, whose grand design
Is to guide us to the fountains
 That o'erflow with bliss divine —
Who proclaim the joyful tidings
 Of salvation all around,
Disregard the world's deridings,
 And in works of love abound.

3 With my substance I will honor
 My Redeemer and my Lord;
Were ten thousand worlds my manor,
 All were nothing to his word:
While the heralds of salvation
 His abounding grace proclaim,
Let his friends, of every station,
 Gladly join to spread his fame.

362 (764) 8s & 7s.   SIGOURNEY.

Missionaries Charged.

ONWARD, onward, men of heaven;
 Bear the gospel banner high;
Rest not till its light is given —
 Star of every pagan sky:
Send it where the pilgrim stranger
 Faints beneath the torrid ray;
Bid the hardy forest-ranger
 Hail it, ere he fades away.

2 Where the Arctic Ocean thunders,
 Where the tropics fiercely glow,
Broadly spread its page of wonders,
 Brightly bid its radiance flow:
India marks its lustre stealing;
 Shiv'ring Greenland loves its rays;
Afric, 'mid her deserts kneeling,
 Lifts the untaught strain of praise.

3 Rude in speech, or wild in feature,
 Dark in spirit, though they be, —
Show that light to every creature,
 Prince or vassal, bond or free:
Lo! they haste to every nation;
 Host on host the ranks supply:
Onward! Christ is your salvation,
 And your death is victory.

363 (744) L. M. WATTS.

Psalm cxvii.

FROM all that dwell below the skies,
Let the Creator's praise arise,—
Let the Redeemer's name be sung
Through every land, by every tongue.

2 Eternal are thy mercies, Lord,
Eternal truth attends thy word;
Thy praise shall sound from shore to
shore
Till suns shall rise and set no more.

364 (607) S. M.

Eccles. xi. 6.

SOW in the morn thy seed,
At eve hold not thy hand;
To doubt and fear give thou no heed —
Broadcast it o'er the land.

2 Beside all waters sow,
The highway furrows stock,
Drop it where thorns and thistles grow;
Scatter it on the rock.

3 The good, the fruitful ground,
Expect not here nor there;
O'er hill, o'er dale, by plots, 't is found:
Go forth, then, everywhere.

4 Thou know'st not which shall thrive,
The late or early sown;
Grace keeps the precious germ alive,
When and wherever strown:

5 And duly shall appear,
In verdure, beauty, strength,
The tender blade, the stalk, the ear,
And the full corn at length.

6 Thou canst not toil in vain:
Cold, heat, and moist, and dry,
Shall foster and mature the grain
For garners in the sky:

7 Thence, when the final end,
The day of God is come,
The angel reapers shall descend,
And heaven sing, " Harvest home !"

365 (760) 7s & 6s. HEBER.

" Come over — and help us."

FROM Greenland's icy mountains,
From India's coral strand;

Where Afric's sunny fountains
Roll down their golden sand;
From many an ancient river,
From many a palmy plain,
They call us to deliver
Their land from error's chain.

2 What though the spicy breezes
Blow soft o'er Ceylon's isle,
Though every prospect pleases,
And only man is vile; —
In vain with lavish kindness
The gifts of God are strown;
The heathen in his blindness
Bows down to wood and stone.

3 Shall we whose souls are lighted
With wisdom from on high,
Shall we to men benighted
The lamp of life deny?
Salvation! O, salvation!
The joyful sound proclaim,
Till earth's remotest nation
Has learned Messiah's name.

4 Waft, waft, ye winds, his story,
And you, ye waters, roll,
Till, like a sea of glory,
It spreads from pole to pole:
Till o'er our ransomed nature,
The Lamb for sinners slain,
Redeemer, King, Creator,
In bliss returns to reign.

366 (756) 8s,7s,&4s. P. WILLIAMS.

Spread of the Gospel.

O'ER the gloomy hills of darkness,
Look, my soul, be still and gaze;
All the promises do travail
With a glorious day of grace:
Blessed jub'lee,
Let thy glorious morning dawn !

2 Kingdoms wide that sit in darkness,
Grant them, Lord, the glorious light;
And from eastern coast to western,
May the morning chase the night;
And redemption,
Freely purchased, win the day.

3 Fly abroad, thou mighty gospel;
Win and conquer, never cease;
May thy lasting, wide dominions,
Multiply, and still increase:
Sway thy sceptre,
Saviour, all the world around.

VI. BIBLE.

367 (770) L. M.   WATTS.
Psalm xix.

THE heavens declare thy glory, Lord,
   In every star thy wisdom shines;
But when our eyes behold thy word,
We read thy name in fairer lines.

2 The rolling sun, the changing light,
   And night and day, thy power confess;
But the blest volume thou hast writ,
   Reveals thy justice and thy grace.

3 Sun, moon, and stars, convey thy praise
   Round the whole earth, and never
      stand;
So when thy truth began its race,
   It touched and glanced on every land.

4 Nor shall thy spreading gospel rest,
   Till through the world thy truth has
      run:
Till Christ has all the nations blessed,
   That see the light, or feel the sun.

368 (775) C. M.   STEELE.
Delighting in the Word.

FATHER of mercies, in thy word
   What endless glory shines!
For ever be thy name adored
   For these celestial lines.

2 Here may the wretched sons of want
   Exhaustless riches find,
Riches above what earth can grant,
   And lasting as the mind.

3 Here the fair tree of knowledge grows,
   And yields a free repast,
Sublimer sweets than nature knows
   Invite the longing taste.

4 Here the Redeemer's welcome voice
   Spreads heavenly peace around;
And life, and everlasting joys,
   Attend the blissful sound.

5 O may these heavenly pages be
   My ever dear delight;
And still new beauties may I see,
   And still increasing light!

12*

VII. CHURCH DEDICATION.

369 (784) L. M.   PALMER.
Dedication.

BEHOLD thy temple, God of grace,
   The house that we have reared for
      thee,
Regard it as thy resting-place,
   And fill it with thy majesty.

2 When from its altar shall arise
   Joint supplication to thy name,
Deign to accept the sacrifice,
   Thyself our answering God proclaim.

3 And when from hence the voice of praise
   Shall lift its triumphs to thy throne,
Show thy acceptance of our lays,
   By making all thy glory known.

4 When here thy ministers shall stand,
   To speak what thou shalt bid them say,
Maintain thy cause with thine own hand,
   And give thy truth a winning way.

370 (785) 7s.   MONTGOMERY.
Dedication.

LORD of hosts, to thee we raise
   Here a house of prayer and praise;
Thou thy people's hearts prepare
Here to meet with praise and prayer.

2 Let the living here be fed
   With thy word, the heavenly bread;
Here, in hope of glory blest,
   May the dead be laid to rest; —

3 Here to thee a temple stand,
   While the sea shall gird the land;
Here reveal thy mercy sure,
   While the sun and moon endure.

4 Hallelujah, — earth and sky
   To the joyful sound reply;
Hallelujah! — hence ascend
   Prayer and praise till time shall end.

ATHENS. C. M. Double. GIARDINI.

VIII. SEASONS.

371 (821) C. M. BROWNE.

End of the Year.

AND now, my soul, another year
Of thy short life is past;
I cannot long continue here,
And this may be my last.

2 Awake, my soul! with utmost care
Thy true condition learn:
What are thy hopes? how sure? how fair?
What is thy great concern?

3 Behold, another year begins!
Set out afresh for heaven;
Seek pardon for thy former sins,
In Christ so freely given.

4 Devoutly yield thyself to God,
And on his grace depend;
With zeal pursue the heavenly road,
Nor doubt a happy end.

372 (808) C. M. C. WESLEY.

New Year's Day.

SING to the great Jehovah's praise!
All praise to him belongs,
Who kindly lengthens out our days,
Demands our choicest songs:
His providence hath brought us through
Another various year;
We all with vows and anthems new
Before our God appear.

2 Father, thy mercies past we own,
Thy still continued care:
To thee presenting, through thy Son,
Whate'er we have or are:
Our lips and lives shall gladly show
The wonders of thy love,
While on in Jesus' steps we go
To seek thy face above.

WARSAW. 6s & 8s.

T. CLARK.

373 (804) 6s & 8s. C. WESLEY.
New Year's Day.

THE Lord of earth and sky,
  The God of ages praise!
Who reigns enthroned on high,
  Ancient of endless days!
Who lengthens out our trials here,
And spares us yet another year.

2 Barren and withered trees,
  We cumbered long the ground!
No fruit of holiness
  On our dead souls was found;
Yet doth he us in mercy spare
Another and another year.

3 When justice gave the word
  To cut the fig-tree down,
The pity of the Lord
  Cried, "Let it still alone!"
The Father mild inclines his ear,
And spares us yet another year.

4 Jesus, thy speaking blood
  From God obtained the grace;
Who therefore hath bestowed
  On us a longer space;
Thou didst in our behalf appear,
And lo! we see another year!

5 Then dig about the root,
  Break up our fallow ground,
And let our gracious fruit
  To thy great praise abound:
O let us all thy praise declare,
And fruit unto perfection bear!

374 (317) 6s & 8s.
Opening Morning Service.

WELCOME, delightful morn,
  Thou day of sacred rest;
I hail thy kind return!
  Lord, make these moments blest.
From the low train of mortal toys
I soar to reach immortal joys.

2 Now may the King descend,
  And fill his throne of grace;
Thy sceptre, Lord, extend,
  While saints address thy face:
Let sinners feel thy quick'ning word,
And learn to know and fear the Lord.

3 Descend, celestial Dove,
  With all thy quick'ning powers;
Disclose a Saviour's love,
  And bless the sacred hours:
Then shall my soul new life obtain,
Nor sabbaths be indulged in vain.

375 (806) C. M. DODDRIDGE.
New Year's Day.

REMARK, my soul, the narrow bound
  Of the revolving year;
How swift the weeks complete their
    round!
How short the months appear!

2 So fast eternity comes on —
  And that important day,
When all that mortal life hath done,
  God's judgment shall survey.

3 Yet, like an idle tale, we pass
  The swift-advancing year;
And study artful ways t' increase
  The speed of its career.

4 Waken, O God, my careless heart,
  Its great concern to see,
That I may act the Christian part,
  To give the year to thee.

376 (807) 7s. NEWTON.
New Year's Day. — Before Sermon.

WHILE with ceaseless course the sun
  Hasted through the former year,
Many souls their race have run,
Never more to meet us here:
Fixed in an eternal state,
They have done with all below;
We a little longer wait,
But how little, none can know.

2 As the wingèd arrow flies
Speedily the mark to find,—
As the lightning from the skies
Darts and leaves no trace behind,—
Swiftly thus our fleeting days
Bear us down life's rapid stream:
Upward, Lord, our spirits raise,
All below is but a dream.

3 Thanks for mercies past receive;
  Pardon of our sins renew;
Teach us henceforth how to live
  With eternity in view:
Bless thy word to young and old,
  Fill us with a Saviour's love;
And when life's short tale is told,
  May we dwell with thee above.

IX. "ORPHANS' HOME."
377 (801) C. M. C. WESLEY.
Anniversary of an Orphan Asylum.

AGAIN the kind revolving year
  Has brought this happy day,
And we in God's blest house appear
  Again our vow to pay.

2 Our watchful guardians, robed in light,
  Adore the heavenly King;
Ten thousand thousand seraphs bright
  Incessant praises sing.

3 They know no want, they feel no care,
  Nor ever sigh as we;
Sorrow and sin are strangers there,
  And all is harmony.

4 If aught can there enhance their bliss,
  Or raise their raptures higher,
New joys in heaven at sights like this,
  New anthems fill the choir.

5 With what resembling care and love
  Both worlds for us appear: —
Our friendly guardians, those above,
  Our benefactors, here.

378 (802) C. M. BROWNE.
Pleading for the Orphan.

O HOW can they look up to heaven,
  And ask for mercy there,
Who never soothed the poor man's pang,
  Nor dried the orphan's tear!

2 The dread omnipotence of Heaven
  We every hour provoke!
Yet still the mercy of our God
  Withholds th' avenging stroke:

3 And Christ was still the healing friend
  Of poverty and pain;
And never did imploring wretch
  His garment touch in vain.

4 May we with humble effort take
  Example from above;
And thence the active lesson learn
  Of charity and love!

379 (869) S. M.   C. WESLEY.
Opening the Exercises.

JESUS, we look to thee,
  Thy promised presence claim;
Thou in the midst of us shalt be,
Assembled in thy name :
Thy name salvation is,
  Which here we come to prove;
Thy name is life, and health, and peace,
And everlasting love.

2 Not in the name of pride
  Or selfishness we meet :
From nature's paths we turn aside,
  And worldly thoughts forget :
We meet the grace to take,
  Which thou hast freely given;
We meet on earth for thy dear sake,
That we may meet in heaven.

3 Present we know thou art ;   •
  But, O, thyself reveal !
Now, Lord, let every bounding heart
  The mighty comfort feel !
O may thy quick'ning voice
  The death of sin remove;
And bid our inmost souls rejoice
In hope of perfect love !

380 (230) S. M.   WATTS.
Psalm xlviii. 10–14.

FAR as thy name is known,
  The world declares thy praise :
Thy saints, O Lord, before thy throne
Their songs of honor raise.

2 With joy let Judah stand
  On Zion's chosen hill,
Proclaim the wonders of thy hand,
  And counsels of thy will.

3 Let strangers walk around
  The city where we dwell;
Compass and view the holy ground,
  And mark the building well —

4 The order of thy house,
  The worship of thy court,
The cheerful songs, the solemn vows, —
  And make a fair report.

5 How decent and how wise!
  How glorious to behold !
Beyond the pomp that charms the eyes,
And rites adorned with gold.

381 (272) S. M.   C. WESLEY.
Opening Conference.

AND are we yet alive,
  And see each other's face ;
Glory and praise to Jesus give
  For his redeeming grace !
Preserved by power divine
  To full salvation here,
Again in Jesus' praise we join,
  And in his sight appear.

2 What troubles have we seen,
  What conflicts have we past,
Fightings without, and fears within,
  Since we assembled last ;
But out of all the Lord
  Hath brought us by his love;
And still he doth his help afford,
  And hides our life above.

3 Then let us make our boast
  Of his redeeming power,
Which saves us to the uttermost,
  Till we can sin no more :
Let us take up the cross,
  Till we the crown obtain ;
And gladly reckon all things loss,
  So we may Jesus gain.

382 (245) S. M. •   C. WESLEY.
The Church Militant.

JESUS, the Conqu'ror, reigns,
  In glorious strength arrayed,
His kingdom over all maintains,
  And bids the earth be glad !

2 Ye sons of men, rejoice
  In Jesus' mighty love :
Lift up your heart, lift up your voice,
  To Him who rules above.

3 Extol his kingly power ;
  Kiss the exalted Son,
Who died, and lives to die no more,
  High on his Father's throne :

4 Our Advocate with God,
  He undertakes our cause,
And spreads through all the earth abroad
  The vict'ry of his cross.

5 That bloody banner see,
  And, in your Captain's sight,
Fight the good fight of faith with me,
  My fellow-soldiers, fight.

AZMON. C. M.

Slow and soft.

383 (904) C. M.   C. WESLEY.

Mutual Aid.

TRY us, O God, and search the ground
  Of every sinful heart:
Whate'er of sin in us is found,
  O bid it all depart !

2 When to the right or left we stray,
  Leave us not comfortless :
But guide our feet into the way
  Of everlasting peace.

3 Help us to help each other, Lord,
  Each other's cross to bear;
Let each his friendly aid afford,
  And feel his brother's care.

4 Help us to build each other up,
  Our little stock improve:
Increase our faith, confirm our hope,
  And perfect us in love.

5 Up into thee, our living Head,
  Let us in all things grow;
Till thou hast made us free indeed,
  And spotless here below.

6 Then, when the mighty work is wrought,
  Receive thy ready bride:
Give us in heaven a happy lot
  With all the sanctified.

384 (916) C. M.   C. WESLEY.

Opening the Exercises.

SEE, Jesus, thy disciples see,
  The promised blessing give !
Met in thy name, we look to thee,
  Expecting to receive.

2 Thee we expect, our faithful Lord,
  Who in thy name are joined ;
We wait according to thy word,
  Thee in the midst to find.

3 With us thou art assembled here,
  But O thyself reveal !
Son of the living God, appear !
  Let us thy presence feel.

4 Breathe on us, Lord, in this our day,
  And these dry bones shall live ;
Speak peace into our hearts, and say,
  " The Holy Ghost receive."

5 Whom now we seek, O may we meet
  Jesus, the Crucified ;
Show us thy bleeding hands and feet,
  Thou who for us hast died.

6 Cause us the record to receive!
  Speak, and the tokens show,
" O be not faithless, but believe
  In me, who died for you ! "

385 (236) C. M. WATTS.
Psalm lxxxix. 15-18.

BLEST are the souls who hear and
know
The gospel's joyful sound;
Peace shall attend the paths they go,
And light their steps surround.

2 Their joy shall bear their spirits up,
Through their Redeemer's name;
His righteousness exalts their hope;
Nor Satan dares condemn.

3 The Lord, our glory and defence,
Strength and salvation gives:
Israel, thy King for ever reigns,
Thy God for ever lives.

386 (237) L. M. WATTS.
Psalm xcii. 12-15.

LORD, 't is a pleasant thing to stand
In gardens planted by thy hand;
Let me within thy courts be seen,
Like a young cedar, fresh and green.

2 There grow thy saints in faith and love,
Blest with thine influence from above;
Not Lebanon, with all its trees,
Yields such a comely sight as these.

3 Laden with fruits of age, they show
The Lord is holy, just, and true:
None that attend his gates shall find
A God unfaithful or unkind.

387 (246) S. M. C. WESLEY.
The Church Militant.

URGE on your rapid course,
Ye blood-besprinkled bands;
The heavenly kingdom suffers force;
'T is seized by violent hands.

2 See there the starry crown
That glitters through the skies!
Satan, the world, and sin, tread down,
And take the glorious prize!

3 Through much distress and pain,
Through many a conflict here,
Through blood, ye must the entrance
gain,
Yet O, disdain to fear.

4 "Courage!" your Captain cries,
(Who all your toil foreknew,)
"Toil ye shall have; yet all despise,
I have o'ercome for you."

388 (250) L. M. C. WESLEY.
Isaiah lii. 1-12.

AWAKE, Jerusalem, awake!
No longer in thy sins lie down;
The garment of salvation take,
Thy beauty and thy strength put on.

2 Shake off the dust that blinds thy sight,
And hides the promise from thine eyes;
Arise, and struggle into light,
The great Deliv'rer calls, Arise!

3 Shake off the bands of sad despair,
Sion, assert thy liberty;
Look up, thy broken heart prepare,
And God shall set the captive free.

4 Vessels of mercy, sons of grace,
Be purged from every sinful stain,
Be like your Lord, his word embrace,
Nor bear his hallowed name in vain.

5 The Lord shall in your front appear,
And lead the pompous triumph on;
His glory shall bring up the rear,
And perfect what his grace begun.

389 (261) L. M. J. WESLEY.
[From the German.]
Laborers.

HIGH on his everlasting throne,
The King of saints his work sur-
veys,
Marks the dear souls he calls his own,
And smiles on the peculiar race.

2 He rests well pleased their toils to see;
Beneath his easy yoke they move;
With all their heart and strength agree
In the sweet labor of his love.

3 See, where the servants of their God,
A busy multitude, appear:
For Jesus day and night employed,
His heritage they toil to clear.

4 The love of Christ their hearts constrains,
And strengthens their unwearied
hands;
They spend their sweat, and blood, and
pains,
To cultivate Immanuel's lands.

5 O multiply thy sowers' seed,
And fruit we every hour shall bear:
Throughout the world thy gospel spread,
Thine everlasting truth declare!

PARK STREET. L. M.

390 (234) L. M.   WATTS.

Psalm lxxxiv. 8–12.

GREAT God, attend while Zion sings
  The joy that from thy presence
    springs:
To spend one day with thee on earth
Exceeds a thousand days of mirth.

2 Might I enjoy the meanest place
Within thy house, O God of grace,
Not tents of ease, nor thrones of power,
Should tempt my feet to leave thy door.

3 God is our sun, he makes our day:
God is our shield, he guards our way
From all th' assaults of hell and sin —
From foes without, and foes within.

4 All needful grace will God bestow,
And crown that grace with glory too:
He gives us all things, and withholds
No real good from upright souls.

5 O God our King, whose sovereign sway
The glorious hosts of heaven obey,
And devils at thy presence flee,
Blest is the man that trusts in thee.

391 (249) L. M.   C. WESLEY.

Isaiah li. 9–11.

ARM of the Lord, awake, awake!
  Thine own immortal strength put on!
With terror clothed, hell's kingdom
    shake,
And cast thy foes with fury down.

2 As in the ancient days, appear!
The sacred annals speak thy fame;
Be now omnipotently near,
To endless ages still the same.

3 By death and hell pursued in vain,
To thee the ransomed seed shall come;
Shouting, their heavenly Sion gain,
And pass through death triumphant
    home.

4 The pain of life shall then be o'er,
The anguish and distracting care;
There sighing grief shall weep no more,
And sin shall never enter there.

5 Where pure, essential joy is found,
The Lord's redeemed their heads shall
    raise,
With everlasting gladness crowned,
And filled with love, and lost in praise.

392 (589) L. M.   HART.
Prayer.

PRAYER is appointed to convey
The blessings God designs to give :
Long as they live should Christians pray,
They learn to pray when first they live.

2 If pain afflict, or wrongs oppress;
If cares distract, or fears dismay;
If guilt deject; if sin distress; —
In every case, still watch and pray.

3 'Tis prayer supports the soul that's weak,
Though thought be broken, language lame,
Pray if thou canst or canst not speak,
But pray with faith in Jesus' name.

4 Depend on him; thou canst not fail;
Make all thy wants and wishes known;
Fear not; his merits must prevail;
Ask but in faith, it shall be done.

393 (591) C. M.   HART.
Opening Worship.

ONCE more we come before our God ;
Once more his blessings ask :
O may not duty seem a load,
Nor worship prove a task !

2 Father, thy quick'ning Spirit send
From heaven in Jesus' name,
To make our waiting minds attend,
And put our souls in frame.

3 May we receive the word we hear,
Each in an honest heart ;
And keep the precious treasure there,
And never with it part.

4 To seek thee all our hearts dispose,
To each thy blessings suit,·
And let the seed thy servant sows
Produce abundant fruit.

394 (592) 7s.   HAMMOND.
Opening Worship.

LORD, we come before thee now,
At thy feet we humbly bow ;
O! do not our suit disdain :
Shall we seek thee, Lord, in vain?

13   K

2 Lord, on thee our souls depend ;
In compassion now descend ;
Fill our hearts with thy rich grace,
Tune our lips to sing thy praise.

3 In thine own appointed way,
Now we seek thee, here we stay ;
Lord, we know not how to go
Till a blessing thou bestow.

4 Send some message from thy word,
That may joy and peace afford ;
Let thy Spirit now impart
Full salvation to each heart.

5 Comfort those who weep and mourn,
Let the time of joy return ;
Those that are cast down lift up,
Make them strong in faith and hope.

6 Grant that all may seek and find
Thee a gracious God, and kind ;
Heal the sick, the captive free ;
Let us all rejoice in thee.

395 (594) S. M.   DODDRIDGE.
Luke xii. 35-37.

YE servants of the Lord,
Each in his office wait,
Observant of his heavenly word,
And watchful at his gate.

2 Let all your lamps be bright,
And trim the golden flame ;
Gird up your loins, as in his sight,
For awful is his name.

3 Watch, 'tis your Lord's command ;
And while we speak he's near ;
Mark the first signal of his hand,
And ready all appear.

4 O happy servant he
In such a posture found !
He shall his Lord with rapture see,
And be with honor crowned.

WATCHMAN. S. M.

396 (912) S. M.   C. WESLEY.

Opening the Exercises.

THE praying spirit breathe,
   The watching power impart;
From all entanglements beneath
   Call off my anxious heart;
My feeble mind sustain,
   By worldly thoughts oppressed;
Appear, and bid me turn again
   To my eternal rest.

2 Swift to my rescue come,
   Thine own this moment seize;
Gather my wand'ring spirit home,
   And keep in perfect peace:
Suffered no more to rove
   O'er all the earth abroad,
Arrest the pris'ner of thy love,
   And shut me up in God.

397 (590) S. M.

" Praying always, with all prayer."

TO God your every want
   In instant prayer display:
Pray always; pray, and never faint;
   Pray, without ceasing, pray.

2 In fellowship, — alone —
   To God with faith draw near:
Approach his courts, besiege his throne,
   With all the power of prayer:

3 Go to his temple, go,
   Nor from his altar move:
Let every house his worship know,
   And every heart his love.

4 To God your spirits dart;
   Your souls in words declare;
Or groan to him who reads the heart,
   Th' unutterable prayer;

5 His mercy now implore;
   And now show forth his praise;
In shouts, or silent awe, adore
   His miracles of grace.

6 Pour out your souls to God,
   And bow them with your knees;
And spread your hearts and hands abroad,
   And pray for Sion's peace.

7 Your guides and brethren bear
   For ever on your mind;
Extend the arms of mighty prayer,
   In grasping all mankind.

DEVOTION. 7s. Double. SPANISH.

398 (871) 7s. C. WESLEY.

Opening the Exercises.

GLORY be to God above,
God from whom all blessings flow;
Make we mention of his love,
Publish we his praise below:
Called together by his grace,
We are met in Jesus' name;
See with joy each other's face,
Foll'wers of the bleeding Lamb.

2 Let us, then, sweet counsel take,
How to make our calling sure,—
Our election how to make,
Past the reach of hell, secure:
Build we each the other up;
Pray we for our faith's increase,
Solid comfort, settled hope,
Constant joy and lasting peace.

399 (877) 7s. C. WESLEY.

Love-feast.

COME, and let us sweetly join,
Christ to praise in hymns divine:
Give we all with one accord
Glory to our common Lord;
Hands, and hearts, and voices, raise;
Sing as in the ancient days;
Antedate the joys above;
Celebrate the feast of love.

2 Strive we, in affection strive;
Let the purer flame revive,
Such as in the martyrs glowed,
Dying champions for their God.
We for Christ our Master stand,
Lights in a benighted land;
We our dying Lord confess,
We are Jesus' witnesses.

400 (878) 7s. C. WESLEY.

Continued.

COME, thou high and lofty Lord!
Lowly, meek, incarnate Word:
Humbly stoop to earth again;
Come and visit abject man!
Jesus, dear expected guest,
Thou art bidden to the feast:
For thyself our hearts prepare:
Come, and sit, and banquet there!

2 Jesus, we thy promise claim:
We are met in thy great name:
In the midst do thou appear,
Manifest thy presence here!
Sanctify us, Lord, and bless!
Breathe thy Spirit, give thy peace;
Thou thyself within us move:
Make our feast a feast of love.

401 (828) C. M.   C. WESLEY.

Renewing the Covenant.

COME, let us use the grace divine,
And all, with one accord,
In a perpetual cov'nant join
Ourselves to Christ the Lord ; —

2 Give up ourselves, through Jesus' power,
His name to glorify ;
And promise, in this sacred hour,
For God to live and die.

3 The cov'nant we this moment make,
Be ever kept in mind :
We will no more our God forsake,
Or cast his words behind.

4 We never will throw off his fear,
Who hears our solemn vow ;
And if thou art well pleased to hear,
Come down, and meet us now !

5 Thee, Father, Son, and Holy Ghost,
Let all our hearts receive ;
Present with the celestial host,
The peaceful answer give.

6 To each the cov'nant blood apply,
Which takes our sins away;
And register our names on high,
And keep us to that day.

402 (882) C. M.   DODDRIDGE.

Admission into the Church.

INQUIRE, ye pilgrims, for the way
That leads to Sion's hill,
And thither set your steady face,
With a determined will.

2 Invite the strangers all around
Your pious march to join ;
And spread the sentiments you feel
Of faith and love divine.

3 O come, and to his temple haste,
And seek his favor there ;
Before his footstool humbly bow,
And pour your fervent prayer.

4 O come, and join your souls to God
In everlasting bands ;
Accept the blessings he bestows,
With thankful hearts and hands.

403 (885) S. M.   MUHLENBERG.

Entering the Ark.

LIKE Noah's weary dove,
That soared the earth around,
But not a resting-place above
The cheerless waters found,—

2 O cease, my wand'ring soul,
On restless wing to roam ;
All the wide world, to either pole,
Has not for thee a home.

3 Behold the ark of God,
Behold the open door ;
Hasten to gain that dear abode,
And rove, my soul, no more.

4 There, safe shalt thou abide,
There, sweet shall be thy rest,
And every longing satisfied,
With full salvation blessed.

404 (892) C. M.

Safety in Union.

JESUS, great Shepherd of the sheep,
To thee for help we fly :
Thy little flock in safety keep !
For O, the wolf is nigh !

2 He comes, of hellish malice full,
To scatter, tear, and slay :
He seizes every straggling soul
As his own lawful prey.

3 Us into thy protection take,
And gather with thy arm :
Unless the fold we first forsake,
The wolf can never harm.

4 We laugh to scorn his cruel power,
While by our Shepherd's side :
The sheep he never can devour,
Unless he first divide.

5 O do not suffer him to part
The souls that here agree ;
But make us of one mind and heart,
And keep us one in thee !

6 Together let us sweetly live,
Together let us die ;
And each a starry crown receive,
And reign above the sky.

ST. THOMAS. S. M.

A. WILLIAMS.

405 (887) S. M.   DWIGHT.

Psalm cxxxvii. 5, 6.

I LOVE thy kingdom, Lord,
 The house of thine abode,
The Church our blest Redeemer bought
With his own precious blood.

2 I love thy Church, O God!
 Her walls before thee stand,
Dear as the apple of thine eye,
And graven on thy hand.

3 If e'er to bless her sons
 My voice or hands deny,
These hands let useful skill forsake,
This voice in silence die.

4 If e'er my heart forget
 Her welfare, or her woe,
Let every joy this heart forsake,
And every grief o'erflow.

5 For her my tears shall fall,
 For her my prayers ascend;
To her my cares and toils be given,
Till toils and cares shall end.

6 Beyond my highest joy
 I prize her heavenly ways,
Her sweet communion, solemn vows,
Her hymns of love and praise.
 18 *

406 (908) S. M.   FAWCETT.

Closing the Exercises.

BLEST be the tie that binds
 Our hearts in Christian love:
The fellowship of kindred minds
Is like to that above.

2 Before our Father's throne
 We pour our ardent prayers;
Our fears, our hopes, our aims are one,
Our comforts and our cares.

3 We share our mutual woes;
 Our mutual burdens bear;
And often for each other flows
The sympathizing tear.

4 When we asunder part,
 It gives us inward pain;
But we shall still be joined in heart,
And hope to meet again.

5 This glorious hope revives
 Our courage by the way;
While each in expectation lives,
And longs to see the day.

6 From sorrow, toil, and pain,
 And sin, we shall be free;
And perfect love and friendship reign
Through all eternity.

407 (891) L. M.   C. WESLEY.

For the Lambs of the Flock.

AUTHOR of faith, we seek thy face,
For all who feel thy work begun:
Confirm, and strengthen them in grace,
And bring thy feeblest children on.

2 Thou seest their wants, thou know'st
their names,
Be mindful of thy youngest care;
Be tender of the new-born lambs,
And gently in thy bosom bear.

3 The lion roaring for his prey,
With rav'ning wolves on every side,
Watch over them to tear and slay,
If found one moment from their Guide.

4 In safety lead thy little flock?
From hell, the world, and sin, secure;
And set their feet upon the rock,
And make in thee their goings sure.

408 (899) C. M.   WATTS.

Psalm cxxxiii.

LO! what an entertaining sight
Are brethren who agree!
Brethren whose cheerful hearts unite
In bands of piety!

2 When streams of love, from Christ the
spring,
Descend to every soul,
And heavenly peace, with balmy wing,
Shades and bedews the whole:

3 'T is like the oil, divinely sweet,
On Aaron's rev'rend head;
The trickling drops perfumed his feet,
And o'er his garments spread.

4 'T is pleasant as the morning dews
That fall on Zion's hill;
Where God his mildest glory shows,
And makes his grace distil.

409 (914) L. M.   COWPER.

Opening the Exercises.

WHAT various hindrances we meet
In coming to a mercy-seat!
Yet who that knows the worth of prayer,
But wishes to be often there?

2 Prayer makes the darkened cloud with-
draw;
Prayer climbs the ladder Jacob saw;
Gives exercise to faith and love;
Brings every blessing from above.

3 Restraining prayer, we cease to fight;
Prayer makes the Christian's armor
bright;
And Satan trembles when he sees
The weakest saint upon his knees.

4 Have you no words? Ah! think again:
Words flow apace when you complain,
And fill your fellow-creature's ear
With the sad tale of all your care.

5 Were half the breath thus vainly spent,
To Heaven in supplication sent,
Your cheerful song would oft'ner be,
"Hear what the Lord has done for me."

410 (921) S. M.   C. WESLEY.

Wants.

JESUS, my strength, my hope,
On thee I cast my care,
With humble confidence look up,
And know thou hear'st my prayer.
Give me on thee to wait,
Till I can all things do,
On thee, almighty to create,
Almighty to renew.

2 I want a sober mind,
A self-renouncing will,
That tramples down and casts behind
The baits of pleasing ill;
A soul inured to pain,
To hardship, grief, and loss,
Bold to take up, firm to sustain,
The consecrated cross.

3 I want a godly fear,
A quick-discerning eye,
That looks to thee when sin is near,
And sees the tempter fly;
A spirit still prepared,
And armed with jealous care,
For ever standing on its guard,
And watching unto prayer.

MELODY. C. M.

411 (911) C. M. C. WESLEY.

Opening the Exercises.

SHEPHERD Divine, our wants relieve,
    In this our evil day;
To all thy tempted foll'wers give
The power to watch and pray.

2 Long as our fiery trials last,
    Long as the cross we bear,
O let our souls on thee be cast
In never-ceasing prayer!

3 The spirit of interceding grace
    Give us in faith to claim;
To wrestle till we see thy face,
And know thy hidden name.

4 Till thou thy perfect love impart,
    Till thou thyself bestow,
Be this the cry of every heart—
I will not let thee go:—

5 I will not let thee go unless
    Thou tell thy name to me,
With all thy great salvation bless,
And make me all like thee.

412 (917) C. M. MONTGOMERY.

What is Prayer?

PRAYER is the soul's sincere desire,
    Uttered or unexpressed;
The motion of a hidden fire
That trembles in the breast.

2 Prayer is the burden of a sigh,
    The falling of a tear;
The upward glancing of an eye,
When none but God is near.

3 Prayer is the simplest form of speech
    That infant lips can try;
Prayer, the sublimest strains that reach
The Majesty on high.

4 Prayer is the Christian's vital breath,
    The Christian's native air;
His watchword at the gates of death;
He enters heaven with prayer.

5 Prayer is the contrite sinner's voice,
    Returning from his ways,
While angels in their songs rejoice,
And cry, "Behold, he prays!"

UXBRIDGE. L. M.

X. FAMILY WORSHIP.

413 (951) L. M. KEN.

Morning.

AWAKE, my soul, and with the sun
　Thy daily stage of duty run;
Shake off dull sloth, and early rise
To pay thy morning sacrifice.

2 Wake and lift up thyself, my heart,
And with the angels bear thy part;
Who all night long unwearied sing
High praise to the eternal King.

3 Glory to thee, who safe hast kept,
And hast refreshed me while I slept:
Grant, Lord, when I from death shall
　　wake,
I may of endless life partake.

4 Direct, control, suggest this day,
All I design, or do, or say,
That all my powers, with all their
　　might,
In thy sole glory may unite.

Praise God, from whom all blessings
　　flow;
Praise him, all creatures here below;
Praise him above, ye heavenly host;
Praise Father, Son, and Holy Ghost.

414 (957) L. M. WATTS.

Morning.—Psalm iii. 5, 8.

TIRED with the burdens of the day,
　To God I raised an evening cry:
He heard when I began to pray,
And his almighty help was nigh.

2 Supported by his heavenly aid,
I laid me down, and slept secure;
Not death should make my heart afraid,
Though I should wake and rise no
　　more.

3 But God sustained me all the night:
Salvation doth to God belong:
He raised my head to see the light
And make his praise my morning
　　song.

MANOAH. C. M.

415 (953) C. M.   WATTS.

Morning.

ONCE more, my soul, the rising day
  Salutes thy waking eyes;
Once more, my voice, thy tribute pay
  To him that rules the skies.

2 Night unto night his name repeats,
  The day renews the sound,—
Wide as the heavens on which he sits,
  To turn the seasons round.

3 'T is he supports my mortal frame;
  My tongue shall speak his praise:
My sins might rouse his wrath to flame,
  But yet his wrath delays.

4 O God, let all my hours be thine,
  While I enjoy the light!
Then shall my sun in smiles decline,
  And bring a pleasant night.

Doxology.

Now let the Father, and the Son,
  And Spirit be adored,
Where there are works to make him
    known,
Or saints to love the Lord.

416 (956) C. M.   DODDRIDGE.

Morning.

AWAKE, my soul, to meet the day,
  Unfold thy drowsy eyes,
And burst the pond'rous chain that loads
  Thine active faculties.

2 God's guardian shield was round me
    spread
In my defenceless sleep:
Let him have all my waking hours
  Who doth my slumbers keep.

3 Pardon, O God, my former sloth,
  And arm my soul with grace;
As rising now, I seal my vows
  To prosecute thy ways.

4 Bright Sun of righteousness, arise;
  Thy radiant beams display,
And guide my dark, bewildered soul
  To everlasting day.

Doxology.

Now let the Father, and the Son,
  And Spirit be adored,
Where there are works to make him
    known,
Or saints to love the Lord.

417 (955) S. M.   SCOTT.

Morning.

SEE how the morning sun
   Pursues his shining way,
And wide proclaims his Maker's praise,
   With every bright'ning ray.

2 Thus would my rising soul
   Its heavenly Parent sing;
And to its great Original
   The humble tribute bring.

3 Serene I laid me down,
   Beneath his guardian care;
I slept, and I awoke, and found
   My kind Preserver near!

4 My life I would anew
   Devote, O Lord, to thee;
And in thy service I would spend
   A long eternity.

418 (973) L. M.   WATTS.

Morning or Evening.

MY God, how endless is thy love!
   Thy gifts are every evening new;
And morning mercies from above
   Gently distil like early dew.

2 Thou spread'st the curtains of the night,
   Great Guardian of my sleeping hours;
Thy sovereign word restores the light,
   And quickens all my drowsy powers.

3 I yield myself to thy command;
   To thee devote my nights and days:
Perpetual blessings from thy hand
   Demand perpetual songs of praise.

419 (974) C. M.   WATTS.

Morning or Evening.

HOSANNA, with a cheerful sound,
   To God's upholding hand!
Ten thousand snares attend us round,
   And yet secure we stand.

2 God is our Sun, whose daily light
   Our joy and safety brings;
Our feeble flesh lies safe at night
   Beneath his shady wings.

420 (952) S. M.

Morning.

WE lift our hearts to thee,
   O Day-Star from on high!
The sun itself is but thy shade,
   Yet cheers both earth and sky.

2 O let thy orient beams
   The night of sin disperse,
The mists of error and of vice
   Which shade the universe!

3 How beauteous nature now!
   How dark and sad before!
With joy we view the pleasing change,
   And nature's God adore.

4 O may no gloomy crime
   Pollute the rising day;
Or Jesus' blood, like evening dew,
   Wash all its stains away!

5 May we this life improve,
   To mourn for errors past,—
And live this short, revolving day
   As if it were our last.

6 To God, the Father, Son,
   And Spirit,—One in Three,—
Be glory; as it was, is now,
   And shall for ever be.

421 (963) S. M.

Evening.

THE day is past and gone,
   The evening shades appear:
O may we all remember well,
   The night of death draws near!

2 We lay our garments by,
   Upon our beds to rest;
So death will soon disrobe us all
   Of what is here possessed.

3 Lord, keep us safe this night,
   Secure from all our fears;
May angels guard us, while we sleep,
   Till morning light appears.

4 And when we early rise,
   And view the unwearied sun,
May we set out to win the prize,
   And after glory run.

MOUNT ZION. L. M.

422 (959) L. M. KEN.
Evening.

ALL praise to thee, my God, this night,
For all the blessings of the light:
Keep me, O keep me, King of kings,
Under thine own Almighty wings.

2 Forgive me, Lord, for thy dear Son,
The ills that I this day have done;
That with the world, myself, and thee,
I, ere I sleep, at peace may be.

3 Teach me to live that I may dread
The grave as little as my bed;
Teach me to die, that so I may
Rise glorious at the awful day.

4 O may my soul on thee repose,
And with sweet sleep mine eyelids close;
Sleep that may me more vig'rous make,
To serve my God, when I awake.

423 (1005) L. M. DODDRIDGE.
Self-examination.

O THOU great God, whose piercing eye
Distinctly marks each deep recess,
In these sequestered hours draw nigh,
And with thy presence fill the place.

2 Through all the mazes of my heart,
My search let heavenly wisdom guide,

And still its radiant beams impart,
Till all be searched and purified.

3 Then with the visits of thy love,
Vouchsafe my inmost soul to cheer;
Till every grace shall join to prove
That God has fixed his dwelling there.

424 (964) L. M. WATTS.
Evening.

THUS far the Lord hath led me on,
Thus far his power prolongs my days,
And every evening shall make known
Some fresh memorial of his grace.

2 Much of my time has run to waste,
And I perhaps am near my home;
But he forgives my follies past,
And gives me strength for days to come.

3 I lay my body down to sleep,
Peace is the pillow for my head;
While well-appointed angels keep
Their watchful stations round my bed.

4 Thus when the night of death shall come,
My flesh shall rest beneath the ground,
And wait thy voice to rouse my tomb,
With sweet salvation in the sound.

AMBOY. 7s, or 8s & 7s.

Small notes to be sung in 8s & 7s.

425 (960) 7s.   C. WESLEY.

Evening.

OMNIPRESENT God! whose aid
   No one ever asked in vain,
Be this night about my bed,
   Every evil thought restrain:
Lay thy hand upon my soul,
   God of my unguarded hours!
All my enemies control,
   Hell, and earth, and nature's powers.

2 O thou jealous God! come down,
   God of spotless purity;
Claim and seize me for thine own,
   Consecrate my heart to thee:
Under thy protection take;
   Songs in the night season give;
Let me sleep to thee, and wake;
   Let me die to thee, and live.

3 Let me of thy life partake,
   Thy own holiness impart;
O that I may sweetly wake,
   With my Saviour in my heart!
O that I may know thee mine!
   O that I may thee receive!
Only live the life divine!
   Only to thy glory live.

426 (961) 8s & 7s.   EDMESTON.

Evening.

SAVIOUR, breathe an evening blessing
   Ere repose our spirits seal;
Sin and want we come confessing;
   Thou canst save and thou canst heal.

2 Though destruction walk around us,
   Though the arrows past us fly,
Angel guards from thee surround us;
   We are safe, if thou art nigh.

3 Though the night be dark and dreary,
   Darkness cannot hide from thee;
Thou art he who, never weary,
   Watcheth where thy people be.

4 Should swift death this night o'ertake us,
   And our couch become our tomb,
May the morn in heaven awake us,
   Clad in light, and deathless bloom.

Doxology.

Praise the Father, earth and heaven,
   Praise the Son, the Spirit praise,
As it was, and is, be given,
   Glory through eternal days.

XI. DOXOLOGIES.

427 (1050) 8s & 7s.
Dismission.

LORD, dismiss us with thy blessing,
  Bid us now depart in peace;
Still on heavenly manna feeding,
  Let our faith and love increase:
Fill each breast with consolation;
  Up to thee our hearts we raise:
When we reach our blissful station,
  Then we'll give thee nobler praise.

GLORIA PATRI.

428 (1052) S. M. WATTS.

GIVE to the Father praise;
  Give glory to the Son;
And to the Spirit of his grace
  Be equal honor done.

429 (1053) C. M. WATTS.

NOW let the Father, and the Son,
  And Spirit be adored,
Where there are works t' make him known,
  Or saints to love the Lord.

430 (1054) L. M. KEN.

PRAISE God, from whom all blessings flow;
Praise him, all creatures here below;
Praise him above, ye heavenly host;
Praise Father, Son, and Holy Ghost.

431 (1061) 7s. C. WESLEY.

SING we to our God above,
  Praise eternal as his love:
Praise him, all ye heavenly host,—
Father, Son, and Holy Ghost.

14

432 10s, 6s, & 8s. (1)
[From "Songs of Zion."]
All is Well.

WHAT'S this that steals, that steals
  upon my frame,—
Is it death, is it death?
That soon will quench, will quench this
  vital flame—
Is it death, is it death?
If this be death, I soon shall be
From every pain and sorrow free,
I shall the King of glory see,—
  All is well, all is well!

2 Weep not, my friends, my friends, weep
    not for me,—
  All is well, all is well:
My sins are pardoned, pardoned, I am
    free,
  All is well, all is well:
There's not a cloud that doth arise
To hide my Jesus from mine eyes:
I soon shall mount the upper skies,—
  All is well, all is well!

3 Tune, tune your harps, your harps, ye
    saints in glory,—
  All is well, all is well!
I will rehearse, rehearse the pleasing
    story,
  All is well, all is well!
Bright angels are from glory come—
They're round my bed, they're in my
    room;
They wait to waft my spirit home,—
  All is well, all is well!

4 Hark, hark! my Lord, my Lord and
    Master calls me,—
  All is well, all is well:
I soon shall see, shall see his face in glory;
  All is well, all is well!
Farewell, my friends, adieu! adieu!
I can no longer stay with you:
My glittering crown appears in view!
  All is well, all is well!

5 Hail! hail! all hail! all hail, you blood-
    washed throng,
  Saved by grace, saved by grace!
I've come to join, to join your rapturous
    song,
  Saved by grace, saved by grace!
All, all is peace and joy divine,
Heaven and glory now are mine,
O hallelujah to the Lamb;
  All is well, all is well!

433   P. M.   (2)
Wondrous Love.

WHAT wondrous love is this, O my
soul! O my soul!
What wondrous love is this, O my soul!
What wondrous love is this, that caused
the Lord of bliss,
To send this precious peace to my soul, to
my soul,
To send this precious peace to my soul.

2 When I was sinking down, etc.,
When I was sinking down, etc.,
When I was sinking down, beneath God's
righteous frown,
Christ laid aside his crown, for my soul,
for my soul,
Christ laid aside his crown, for my soul!

3 Ye friends of Zion's King, join his
praise, etc.,
Ye friends of Zion's King, etc.,
Ye friends of Zion's King, with hearts
and voices sing,
And strike each tuneful string in his
praise, etc.,
And strike each tuneful string in his
praise.

4 To God and to the Lamb, I will sing, etc.,
To God and to the Lamb I will sing,
To God and to the Lamb, who is the great
I AM!
While millions join the theme, I will
sing, etc.,
While millions join the theme, I will
sing.

5 And when from death I'm free, I'll sing
on, etc.,
And when from death I'm free, I'll sing
on,
And when from death I'm free, I'll sing
and joyful be;
And through eternity I'll sing on, etc.,
And through eternity I'll sing on.

434   P. M.   (3)
O When Shall I See Jesus?

O WHEN shall I see Jesus,
And dwell with him above;
To drink the flowing fountain
Of everlasting love?
When shall I be delivered
From this vain world of sin,
And with my blessed Jesus
Drink endless pleasures in?

CHO. O how charming, how charming,
How charming is Jesus,
He is my Redeemer,
My friend and my King.

2 But now I am a soldier,
My Captain's gone before;
He's given me my orders,
And tells me not to fear;
And if I hold out faithful,
A crown of life he'll give,
And all his valiant soldiers
Eternal life shall have.

3 Through grace I am determined
To conquer though I die,
And then away to Jesus
On wings of love I'll fly:
Farewell to sin and sorrow,
I bid you all adieu:
And you, my friends, prove faithful,
And on your way pursue.

4 And if you meet with trials,
And troubles on your way,
Cast all your care on Jesus,
And don't forget to pray:
Gird on the heavenly armor
Of faith, and hope, and love,
And when your race is ended,
You'll reign with him above.

435   C. M.   (4)
Happy Souls.

HAPPY souls! how fast you go,
And 'cave me far behind!
Don't stay for me, for now I see
The Lord is good and kind.

2 Go on, go on, my soul says go,
And I'll come after you:
Though I'm behind, I feel inclined
To sing hosanna too.

3 God give you strength your race to run,
And keep your footsteps right;
Though fast you go, and I so slow,
You are not out of sight.

4 When you get to that world above,
And all God's glory see:
On that bright shore, your journey's o'er,
Then look you out for me.

5 I'm coming on fast as I can,
Nor toil nor danger fear;
God give me strength, may I at length
Be one among you there.

6 Then altogether we shall meet,
Together we will sing;
Together we will praise our God
And everlasting King.

436   11s. **(5)**

An Alien from God.

Tune: *Sweet Home.*

AN alien from God, and a stranger to
    grace,
I wander through earth its gay pleasures
    to trace;
In the pathway of sin I continued to
    roam,
Unmindful, alas! that it led me from
    home.
  Home, home, sweet, sweet home,
  O Saviour! direct me to heaven my
    home.

2 The pleasures of earth, I have seen fade
    away,
They bloom for a season, but soon they
    decay,
But pleasures more lasting, in Jesus are
    given,
Salvation on earth, and a mansion in
    heaven.
  Home, home, sweet, sweet home,
  The saints in those mansions are ever
    at home.

3 Allure me no longer, ye false glowing
    charms!
The Saviour invites me, I'll go to his
    arms:
At the Banquet of Mercy, I hear there is
    room,   [home!
O there may I feast with his children at
  Home, home, sweet, sweet home,
  O Jesus conduct me to heaven my
    home!

4 Farewell, vain amusements, my follies
    adieu,   [view;
While Jesus, and heaven, and glory I
I feast on his pleasures that flow from
    his throne,   [my home.
The foretaste of heaven, sweet heaven,
  Home, home, sweet, sweet home,
  O when shall I share the fruition of
    home!

5 The days of my exile are passing away,
The time is approaching when Jesus will
    say:
Well done, faithful servant, sit down on
    my throne,   [home.
And dwell in my presence for ever at
  Home, home, sweet, sweet home,
  O there I shall rest with the Saviour
    at home.

437   11s. **(6)**

From Gloomy Dejection.

Tune: *How firm a foundation.*

FROM gloomy dejection my thoughts
    mount the sky,
And realms ever peaceful, transported
    descry;
There joys ever blooming, enrapture the
    soul,
And rivers of pleasure incessantly roll.

2 There sorrow norsighing can never infest,
Nor Satan harass, nor the wicked molest;
But whererest perpetual the weary obtain,
Their harvest of joy, and their infinite
    gain.

3 Ere long, when those shadows shall all
    be withdrawn,
Extinguished before the glad light of the
    dawn;
Which rises to scatter the mourner's sad
    gloom,
And bury for ever their woes in the tomb.

4 I too shall inherit the heavenly prize,
To scenes of bright glory my soul shall
    arise,
With rapture ineffable join the glad
    throng,   [song.
And, filled with new wonder, unite in the

5 If such be my portion, why should I
    complain?   [retain?
Why cherish despondence, why sadness
Is sorrow then meet for an heir of the
    skies,   [shall rise?
Who shortly to blessings unbounded

6 No longer I'll murmur, no longer repine,
But joy 'midst those troubles, since
    heaven is mine;
Then deep in oblivion be sunk every fear,
Be erased from my bosom each trace of
    despair.

7 How glorious the scheme that grace doth
    enhance,
Our hopes to enliven, our bliss to advance!
It fills me with transport, my joys over-
    flow,
Too big for expression, ecstatic they grow.

8 O aid me, ye angels, its wonders to tell,
Encompass the theme, in full sympathy
    dwell;
But still it enlarges — no angel can scan,
The scheme of redemption, the wonderful
    plan.

438   S. M.   **(7)**

O Sing to me of Heaven.

O SING to me of heaven,
   When I am called to die!
Sing songs of holy ecstasy,
   To waft my soul on high!

2 When cold and sluggish drops
   Roll off my marble brow,
Burst forth in strains of joyfulness,
   Let heaven begin below!

3 When the last moment comes,
   O watch my dying face,
And catch the bright, seraphic gleam
   Which o'er each feature plays.

4 Then, to my ravished ears,
   Let one sweet song be given —
Let music charm me last on earth,
   And greet me first in heaven.

5 Then close my sightless eyes,
   And lay me down to rest,
And clasp my cold and icy hands
   Upon my lifeless breast.

6 Then round my lifeless clay
   Assemble those I love,
And sing of heaven, delightful heaven,
   My glorious home above.

439   8s & 4s.   **(8)**

Vain World, Adieu!

WHEN for eternal worlds we steer,
   And seas are calm and skies are
     clear,
And faith in lively exercise,
And distant hills of Canaan rise,
The soul for joy then claps her wings,
And loud her lovely sonnet sings,
     Vain world, adieu.

2 With cheerful hope her eyes explore
Each landmark on the distant shore:
The trees of life, the pastures green,
The crystal stream — delightful scene!
Again for joy she claps her wings,
And loud her lovely sonnet sings,
     Vain world, adieu.

3 The nearer still she draws to land,
More eager all her powers expand:
With steady helm and free-bent sail,
Her anchor drops within the veil:
Again for joy she claps her wings,
And her celestial sonnet sings,
     Glory to God!

440   **(9)**   6s & 4s.   HUNTER.

Give me Jesus.

WHILE wandering to and fro,
   In this wide world of wo,
Where streams of sorrow flow,
Give me Jesus — give me Jesus — give
   me Jesus —
You may have all this world — give me
   Jesus.

2 When tears o'erflow mine eye,
   When pressed by grief I sigh,
Still this shall be my cry,
   Give me Jesus.

3 When to the mercy-seat
   I go my Lord to meet,
My heart shall still repeat,
   Give me Jesus.

4 And when my faith is tried,
   In him will I confide,
And all the storms outride —
   Give me Jesus.

5 Though strength and friends should fail,
   And foes my soul assail,
Through him I shall prevail —
   Give me Jesus.

6 And when my toils are o'er,
   When nearing Jordan's shore,
I'll shout as up I soar,
   Give me Jesus.

7 When at the judgment-seat,
   I stand at Jesus' feet,
When worlds on worlds shall meet,
   Give me Jesus.

8 When heaven and earth shall flee,
   When time shall cease to be,
Through all eternity,
   Give me Jesus.

THE END.